THE GAME
According to Daddy

A WOMAN'S JOURNEY TO
A SUCCESSFUL RELATIONSHIP

SHON WATTS

Copyright © 2010 by Shon Watts
Cover Art by André David
Book Design by Janna Geary

Published by Up Close and Personal Publishing

Visit our website at: www.closeandpersonalpublishing.com
Printed in the United States of America
ISBN-13 9780615368559
ISBN-10 0615368557

DEDICATION

This book is dedicated to my two daughters. I pray that your journey into womanhood is one of patience, wisdom, fun, and love.

Acknowledgements

This book has truly been an adventure to write. There are just entirely too many people to personally thank, so I'll just keep it short by saying thanks to all my family and close friends for the words of encouragement, without your love and support this would have never came to fruition.

CONTENTS

PROLOGUE

On April 3, 2010, at roughly 9:00 p.m. Central time (two days before opening day of the 2010/2011 baseball season), my youngest child, at the ripe tender age of four, walked up to me with a look of innocence in her face and a book of choice in her hand. She gave me a heart-melting smile that only a father can appreciate getting from his baby girl as he willingly gives in and marvels at how quickly she has learned to use her girlish charms to get what she wants from the first male love of her life.

Her words were soft and playful, and flowed from her mouth in an almost melodic tone: "Daddy, can you read this book to me?" "Of course I will baby girl," I said genuinely as I lifted her up on my lap. "Let me see what we'll be reading," I added playfully as I prepared myself to read something light and childish. You know...maybe something new and contemporary like *Dora the Explorer* or *Elmo's World*. Or perhaps something classic that, for generations, has been a catalyst for causing children to laugh, to wonder, and to dream big infinite dreams that always seem to end with them sleeping happily in your arms, waiting to be carried to their beds in a peaceful slumber, tucked in gently, and kissed a pleasant goodnight. You know what I'm talking about: something nice and safe like *Green Eggs and Ham* or *Goldilocks and the Three Bears*.

But as fate would have it...that was not to be my destiny.

Instead, I was handed the one book for which—as a father and a man—I have always harbored deep, serious disdain. And in that moment, I knew my journey, like the journey of so many fathers before me, had begun.

In my hands I held the one book that, if not corrected early on, could put my baby girl in harm's way by inadvertently placing her on a path to grandiose thoughts and lavish dreams—a path that could forever ruin her chances of finding real happiness and discovering the value of learning to know/love herself before ever coming to value/love a man. In my hand, my daughter had placed my nightmare and, sadly, what for decades has ruined plenty of good women by becoming their warped Twilight Zone fantasy. In my hand was the book known worldwide to most simply as Cinderella, but which was known more commonly to me-and many enlightened men-as "Bullshit!"

And with that...I knew this moment was a transitional moment for both of us. I knew if I failed to do my duty, my daughter—like the daughters of so many others—could end up a *victim*. *Not on my watch!* I uttered quietly to myself. *I've got to do something to make sure she doesn't fall victim to this*, I thought, as I made a mental note to find a way to set *The Game* straight before Ms. Cinderella could firmly plant her venomous seeds into my baby girl's fertile, impressionable imagination. *Not on my watch!* I gasped again. "But, damn, she's only four! Do I ruin her childhood by telling her the truth before it's time? In fact, when's a good time to tell her and how/where shall I begin?" My internal conflict battled on as I turned the pages and began to read the story aloud: "Once upon a time, there lived a girl named Cinderella, who was very beautiful and very kind..." *Not on my watch!* I vowed.

INTRODUCTION

"Never let the fear of striking out keep you from playing the game."
—Unknown

I have a lot of different reasons for deciding to write this book. However, rather than going through the plethora of reasons and having you walk away feeling like you really missed the point, I think it's best to strictly say, "It's time."

As a father, a husband, a son, an uncle, a brother, a friend, a teacher, and so many other titles of relevance that mean so much to so many women I have encountered in my life, I feel the best thing I could do to show how much I love, cherish, and value those relationships is to simply tell you my truth. Though somewhere in the process of reading this, you might find yourself going through a variety of emotions, know that the intent was not to hurt you, but to uplift and inform you so you could ultimately move on to a better place and make better-informed decisions about the men you choose to allow in your life.

I can't say that I'm perfect, nor do I really ever want to lay claim to that title...too much pressure (just ask any of your local male politicians or members of the clergy). But I can say that I love my daughters enough to want them to know about *"The Game,"* how to play it, how to respect it, and how to live their lives in a way that they will get more from it than they lose to it.

Many people may not like my metaphor and how I chose to set up the relevance of my message (especially those people who have decided to live their lives as pious religious fanatics who know "exactly" what God meant to say before He said it and can quote more scriptures than King James, Buddha, Mohammad, and Jesus rolled into one). That's fine. Please know that I didn't write this book for you and you should probably not read it and move on with your life while you still know all the answers. I respect where you're coming from and wish you the best on your journey to happiness, but this is written for MY DAUGHTERS and the women I love. Therefore, I'm entitled to have my say, even if you don't like it and disagree.

With all of that being said, let us start with some simple questions: As a woman, have you found yourself feeling frustrated about men and why we behave the way we do? Have you yearned to have an in-depth conversation with a man you have an interest, hoping that he would be open and honest with you about who he is, where he is in his life, and what his intentions are as it relates to you? Do you find yourself beginning to feel like all men are "dogs" and we have no real place in your life? If these questions have raised a feeling you can relate to and you want to know the answers, come with me and let us embark upon a journey.

This journey will take you to a place where you never thought you would find answers, but will leave you feeling empowered and no longer feeling like a victim. Instead, it is my hope that when we are done with our journey, you will feel more like a *Player* that recognizes where you are in *The Game* and begin making decisions that will allow you to play to win.

This journey begins on a baseball field that can be found in any town in any state/province located in a variety of places throughout the free world. It is a journey that can be called *a game* and is therefore meant to be played...and played it is. It is played under the day or night light, with people watching in the stands, cheering and booing for their favorite player to make a play that will make them the MVP of the game. It has rules/structure, it has offensive/defensive tactics, it has coaches, it has penalties, but most importantly, it has answers. This game is called *baseball* and it has answers to issues about male/female relationships that will change your life's perspective.

1ˢᵀ INNING

I'm sure you're probably sitting there reading this, going: "What the hell does baseball have to do with male/female relationships?" Well, if you really think about it metaphorically, you should begin to see not only its relevance, but their similarities.

In baseball, the whole objective of the game is to hit one of the balls that's pitched to you from the pitcher in such a way that no one will tag you out while you run around the bases trying to get back to home plate to score. Well, in a healthy male/female relationship the objective is generally (at least in most of the ones I'm familiar with) to find the perfect mate and maneuver yourself around the various obstacles that may come your way, so ultimately you will arrive at a life of eternal blissful happiness with that one lifetime partner. In other words, the goal in a relationship, like in baseball, is to hit a HOME RUN and score.

Note: This is the point where some of you will try to become philosophical/over-analytical (you know who you are…the "I know everything" Freudian types). This is where you begin to search for loopholes in the example and rather than simply accepting the simplicity of the metaphor and staying with the theme, you'll say things like, "Well, this is not a good example because in baseball, after you hit a home run the game is not over; you still have to come back up to bat another time." And to you I say, "Stop being the person at the movies that makes it hard for everyone else to enjoy the plot simply because you think you've figured it out in the first three minutes of the film and you ruin it for everyone else by trying to show how brilliant you think you are." Just so you know (and you can act like you didn't hear this from me), "You're the one everyone wants to throw darts at!" Therefore, do us all a favor by simply continuing to read and I'll get you back on track (I hope) soon enough!

Although I will discuss all 10 players on the field (9 on defense on the opposing team and 1 at the plate on offense that's batting), in this metaphor there are 4 players and 1 non-player that will ultimately shape the outcome of *The Game*, how you see yourself as a player, and whether or not you will ever make it to the *Hall of Fame*.

Each of these players plays a crucial role in your game. They each have very distinctive jobs that must be performed flawlessly so the desired outcome is achieved in a successful manner. However, if at some point during *The Game* any of them should fail to do their job, the outcome can be devastating.

2NDINNING

The first VIP position in the game of baseball is called the *First Baseman*, **a.k.a.,** *"The Devirginizer."*

This player is the lead-off man in the game who helps set the tone for how the rest of *The Game* will begin to unfold. If he does his job properly, a woman will be in the proper position to stay on course for running to second, but if he fails to complete his job, she may find herself OUT and never able to fully recover or get her head back into the game.

Before I go on to explain the three important jobs *The Devirginizer* must perform, I have to prep it by saying that it is **imperative** these jobs are performed respectfully and without malice. Unfortunately, they must be performed in such a way that they cause pain, but the crucial part in this job performance is to cause the pain without breaking the spirit; because if the spirit is broken, this starts a woman on a totally different path than the desired outcome—and often this path leads to a place of no return.

In this game, *The Devirginizer's* three distinct jobs are:

- *First, to take the woman's virginity (please know that when I say "take," that's not meant literally as "to take something by force or by extreme manipulative tactics");*
- *Second, to kill the "Cinderella Syndrome";*
- *Third (unfortunately), to break her heart.*

I know some of you are sitting there staring at the pages right now in disbelief. Some of you are probably even cussing and asking yourselves, "Who the hell does this *S^S%# think he is by suggesting something as cruel as this!!" Sorry, ladies, these are all critical steps in learning how to play *The Game* to win and you have to get over the fear of not allowing this to happen to you. Remember: The key to learning to play this game is learning how to make informed decisions so you can have a better understanding of what's going on when it's happening and play a role in how YOU allow it to unfold.

In any game, a person can only do to you what you allow them to do, but if you aren't even aware that you're a *"non-participating member"* in a game, then you are a victim. And victims are only given the choice of receiving what the aggressor dishes out.

Taking the Woman's Virginity

Contrary to many beliefs, the *first baseman* has to be good at several things, but the master of none. He can specialize in any of his required jobs, but he can't be so good at them that he becomes cocky and begins to flaunt his skills.

I know this sounds very systematic, but the reality is that 9 out of 10 times, somebody is eventually going to get it anyway. And more than likely the person that gets it is not going to be the man you told yourself you were going to wait for until you got married.

As a matter of fact, the whole idea of waiting until you're married to have sex needs to be erased from your brain! "Quick! Someone run and grab a cup of water and a fan! Sistah Johnson just fainted!!"

That's right...I said it and I meant it!

Waiting until you're married to have sex is like waiting until you buy a car to test drive it. It may seem like a bold simile, but who wants to get that car home and later find out that it looked good on the outside, but had absolutely no horsepower or performance in the engine? It could go from 0 – 60 in 10 minutes and all it was ever really good for was sitting still at stoplights, looking hot, so people could think it was a great car and wish they had it!

In other words, why would you want to wait until you're married to find out whether or not you're sexually compatible with someone?

Sex is a VERY important part in a healthy relationship. Therefore, too much is on the line for you to go into a marriage having never had any experience in finding out who you are and what pleases you. And if you go into a marriage having never found these things out, how are you ever going to know how to please your man or to have him please you?

I know some people will say, "*Well, we can learn together.*" That's a bunch of crap! Most *males* like the idea of being a woman's first lover, but the reality is when it comes to actually dealing with the emotional instability that comes with it, men (the key word here is "MEN"—25 and older) are generally turned off by it and find it to be more of a headache than an honor. We generally feel it's something you should have dealt with early in your life, between the ages of 18-21 and not have waited until you were 25 to get to it.

Plus (unfortunately), some women have been raised to believe that when they decide to have sex with a man, they are doing him a favor and giving him something that's holier than the tabernacle. That's cute, but just not true.

To be honest, that's a great way of giving your daughter self-esteem and making her aware she has to be conscious of her body and know she does, in fact, have something that should be deemed precious to her (the key words here are *"to her"*). But the reality is her gift is no more precious than the man giving of himself, and therefore when she gives it, she should give it to a man she deems worthy, but not give it thinking it makes him forever obligated to her because she gave it.

This false sense of power has caused a lot of heartache for women, especially when they run across a man who hasn't bought into this philosophy and ultimately bursts their bubble by letting it be known he has brought something to the table she needs/ desires just as much as she has brought something he needs/desires. It's almost mind-blowing to know there are actually women out there who *truly believe* their sex is the best sex in the world and any man that gets it should count himself blessed. Ladies, it can be a hard fall off that mountain, so be careful not to go too high, where the oxygen thins and begins to affect your brain!

The best you can hope for is to find a *first baseman* who sees you as special and takes his time to try to really build a relationship with you on multiple levels. These levels should entail him spending time getting to know you, wanting to know about your dreams/ aspirations, and taking the time to become a friend— someone you can talk to, laugh with, depend on, and when/if the time comes…maybe even cry with. But, ultimately, he must fulfill his mission of doing what his job requires.

REFLECTION

By being the person you chose to give your virginity to, he has hopefully forever stamped a special place in your heart by having made the experience as pleasurable/memorable for you as possible. Hopefully, he was chosen because he was successful in making you feel he would be a considerate lover, actually take his time with you, and never make you feel that if you chose not to give it to him he would take it personally and leave you for someone else.

Note: The reality is, more than likely, he is going to get it from someone else anyway—you're not marrying him, you're just dating him! But he needs to be tactful enough to at least make you feel he's on the up-and-up.

Hopefully, you chose someone who understood his role as your first lover and was raised to actually love/ respect women, and he didn't have a mindset where he felt women are simply slices of succulent sweet meat waiting to be discarded as men deem fit.

Note: This may seem like a contradiction, but believe me, there's a BIG DIFFERENCE between a man who actually loves a woman enough to realize he can only go so far with her in her growth/ development and loves/respects her enough to have the strength to let her go on to her next phase willingly without ruining her, versus a man who despises women to the point where he feels women are really just victims waiting to be pimped and emotionally abused every chance he finds one he can exploit.

Know this: The *first baseman* understands that having sex does not make him your husband nor obligates him to you until death do you part. Therefore, when he begins to pull away after a while and tells you he wants to see other people, begins to slowly find himself having less and less time to hang out with you, or you two ultimately get to a point where you find yourselves arguing over small things more than you find yourselves laughing and having quality time, just know that this too is part of the

10

process and he has moved into phase two of his job: *killing the Cinderella Syndrome.*

KILLING CINDERELLA

The story of Cinderella is a very interesting story, and in my opinion, it has done more psychological damage to women than any other story ever told in the history of storytelling.

It starts off cute and innocent enough: A young poor girl, due to a tragic loss, finds herself alone in the world without a mother. Her father eventually remarries and she becomes part of a family that now encompasses a stepmother and two stepsisters.

On the outside things look good, but the reality is the girl is mistreated from day one because she's seen as an outsider, as well as a threat, because of her natural beauty and innocent charm.

The hook-and-crook of this story's damage comes into play when we begin to talk about how Ms. Cinderella eventually finds herself marrying a prince who has searched his kingdom far and wide looking for her after she initially rejected his power/charm and left him standing on the dance floor feeling horny/hot in her attempt to get home before the stroke of midnight rather than risk the illusion of her fairy godmother's spell wearing off in front of him (when he would see her getting turned back into an ordinary woman instead of the made-up beauty queen he has spent his evening being drawn to and fascinated with).

After finding a piece of her beauty, her glass slipper, to prove she was in fact *real* and not a figment of his imagination, he has his servants search high and wide to locate her so he can ultimately reclaim his one true love. When he eventually finds her, he literally comes along and sweeps her off her feet, begs her to become his Mrs., rescues her from the harsh environment of her evil stepmother/stepsisters, and they live..."Happily Ever After!"

If we take a moment to really examine this story and its elaborate fabricated ending, we can truly see where the damage has left its unyielding red stain on the psyche of women all around the free world and why the *first baseman's* job is pivotal in helping to set *The Game* straight.

First, we have Ms. Cinderella: a domestic, uneducated (but cute) female with nothing else to offer but her youthful innocence and her virginity, and who's coming from a family of domestic abuse and instability. Second, we have an attractive, charming, and well-educated youthful prince who has the world in front of him, along with infinite opportunities to explore, conquer, and see the world.

Because of his youth/power and blind infatuation with Cinderella's spell of beauty/awe, the prince's hormones/pride ultimately make him reject all of the academically/ economically equally suited princesses in the surrounding kingdoms who are not only attracted to him, but open to building a life with him as well. He instead rejects all of their luster and equal power/wealth, and chooses to run after the one cute domestic/uneducated girl he felt got away simply because he got caught up in her looks and she didn't fall victim to his wealth and success.

Now, let us fast forward to the real world, where we see this sick sense of creative psychosis actually being planted into the cerebrums of many girls by their twisted parents.

Believe it or not, there are women out there who are actually being raised to believe that because they're cute (and in many cases might have a big butt, nice body, and a nice smile), some horny, spellbound, infatuated, lame, charming prince is going to come along to blow it all on her, sweep her off her feet away from her troubles, and give her the world simply because she gave up her virginity and decided (oftentimes, without his consent) that he was going to be the man she spends the rest of her life with. Ladies, please WAKE UP! (**Note:** *Lame, charming prince* is a true oxymoron, but in order for this to actually happen on a regular basis in the *real world,* these guys would have to be nothing short of OXYMORONS. And I'm using the word "MORON" very loosely!)

No one ever tells you how, in the *real world,* the prince wakes up one day, after the honeymoon period has worn off, and has an epiphany of what has transpired. They don't tell you how after he has had his fair share of breaking you in, he comes to realize what all he gave up and left on the table for the cute, charming, innocent girl with the nice body, the big butt, and the cute smile who didn't really know herself, hadn't experienced a lot of things in the world, had no real culture or educational background to match his own, came from a broken home, and really brought nothing to the table but dreams of living a life of comfort and being a **dependent**. They don't tell you how, eventually, he gets tired and begins making plans to move on…without you.

Look ladies, I don't want to come across as the butt-hole sibling that pulls you to the side while munching on one of your specially made *Santa-Only* cookies, and sarcastically tells you: "You know, Santa's really not real and Mom and Dad have been hiding toys in the closet for the last week waiting for you to go to bed." But I do want to say it is imperative to be open/honest with women about how men see you and how we view the world. We're very analytical as well as practical in our thinking. We can make decisions that may seem harsh to a sensitive heart, but very logical to us. Therefore, to walk around thinking men will not add up your total value and what you actually bring to the table besides **your cute face, big butt, and nice body** is to do yourself a grave disservice, and it sets you up again to fall even harder from the lofty mountaintop YOU may have placed yourself on.

Therefore, if you have a solid *first baseman* in your life and he knows what he has to do, he will do what is right and destroy this image of you meeting your prince the first time out and living happily ever after. It may hurt, but "that which does not kill you only makes you stronger," and you have to be strong to have longevity to play *The Game* for keeps.

BREAKING YOUR HEART

How does one go about breaking a heart the right way? Is this even a logical question that's worthy of conversation? Believe it or not, I believe it is. There is definitely a method to breaking a heart, but more importantly, there's a valid reason for why the heart has to be broken.

Imagine constantly walking around the world feeling life is grand and nothing ever goes wrong. I'm not sure if people in the adult world would actually take you seriously, but I do know you would find yourself being labeled as someone who needs to grow up and see the world for what it is.

In the *real world*, there's joy/pain, good/bad, as well as life/death…and in order to have a true human experience, unfortunately you have to know them all.

A good *first baseman* will be an intricate part in helping you come out of your mythical illusion of the *"perfect world."* By getting you acclimated to the true ups/downs life has to offer, he will not only hand you your first serious loss, but he will have positioned himself to help prepare you for having the survival skills you'll need later in life when things don't always work out the way you anticipated and hoped for.

We would all like to believe that we will achieve everything we set our minds to—and in rare cases, some people actually pull it off, but they are the exception and not the rule. That's the equivalent of saying you are going to win the million-dollar lottery the first time you ever play. It has been done, but what are the odds of it happening to you, and is that how you want to approach your life…living to try to beat the odds? We would also like to believe that any person we tell ourselves we love will wholeheartedly love us forever in return, but in telling ourselves this, we are lying and refusing to face reality—and people who have a fear of facing reality are in a state of delusion. And the last time I checked, we have mental hospitals, with serious treatment centers, for people who are totally lost in a state of delusion and can't cope with the real world. Therefore, ladies don't fight getting your heart broken. Instead, learn to reflect upon the lessons that come with the heartache and try to grow from it.

If you never slow down to reflect, and simply jump from one relationship to another, you fail to recognize your strengths/weaknesses to see where you need to grow/improve. And when you begin discovering these lessons, pass them on to a friend, a daughter, a niece, or a cousin that has yet to hit the playing field to help her better prepare for the inevitable. This way she'll be better equipped to go into *The Game* having been informed from veteran players and not feel isolated/ destroyed when her turn at bat begins.

Don't become bitter and feel like you want to see others suffer like you. Believe me, everyone has to play *The Game* in one form or another...yes, even men (but that's another book for another day). Therefore, you will not ever be by yourself. You'll simply be sharing your journey to help others begin to prepare for theirs.

CHANGING BASES

When you leave first base, you should come away with some skills in your repertoire that help assure you are indeed ready for the next base. However, if these skills and lessons have not been mastered, you won't be ready when it's time to run to the next base and you'll find yourself being tagged OUT for daydreaming on base and not paying attention to the game being played around you.

You should walk away having learned some things about yourself sexually. In fact, part of the *first baseman's* job is to help you get to a place/space where you begin to feel comfortable expressing your sexuality and knowing how to please not only yourself, but also your partner. (**Note:** No matter what people may say or preach, taking the time to discover who you are and what makes you happy is important to your life's journey. Sadly, there are some people out there—men and women alike—who simply fear the idea of women being as sexual as men. These are people that tell you how it's wrong for a woman to openly embrace being sexual and to realize she too has sexual urges, fantasies, and natural curiosities. But remember, that's the same group I originally said

should not read this book and requested that they go
back to being pious while they are still on God's
"Favorite Persons List.")

Once you get over the initial shock that it actually
happened to YOU and come to see that, yes, you're
human after all—and, like Christ (and all the other
prophets), you too must know pain/suffering—you
should now seize the time to find the lessons in the
relationship.

For instance, reflect on whether or not you chose a
guy that seemed to have some form of compassion
and respect for others. Did you choose someone that
respected you as a person and saw value in you being
more than just a pretty face with a nice body? Did he
take the time to actually take interest in your dreams/
aspirations? Did you choose someone who had
dreams/aspirations of his own and was actually
working toward them, or was he merely good at
talking the talk and never walking the walk? Did he
have respect for his mother and did it carry over to
how he interacted with you? Did he enjoy letting you
see his sensitive side or was he always in *battle mode*
and flexing a false sense of male bravado? Did he have
respect for his father and see him as an example of the
kind of man he aspired to become? Did he actually
invite you into his world and put you on a pedestal
when you were there? Did you choose someone that

had a hard, honest work ethic, or did you choose someone with a *"the world owes me something"* attitude who felt it was better to prey on people before getting preyed upon? When the relationship begin to fade, and it was time for him to move to *the Cinderella phase*, did he exude some form of care/compassion about your feelings, or was he just brutal and told you to, *"Make like Mike and Beat it!"*

These may seem like simple questions, but if you found yourself having chosen someone that was cruel to you, only cared about your outer beauty, didn't give a damn if you had any dreams/aspirations, never engaged you in mental dialogue, felt threatened if you showed your intellectual side, had no real dreams of his own, seemed to be more of a talker than a doer, had a *"the world owes me something"* attitude, and had no respect for his parents or others...you might want to look more deeply at yourself and ask why you would choose that kind of man in the first place! And whatever your reasoning may be for arriving at the point where you saw this kind of man as acceptable, you need to work on adjusting it if you're planning to stay in *The Game* to win.

Generally speaking, women who find they're drawn to certain kinds of men (especially those who demonstrate qualities of being losers) early on in *The Game* and fail to make the required adjustments quickly put themselves on track of possibly running across that **rogue baseman** that will ultimately break their spirit instead of their heart. And as I previously stated, healing a broken spirit may take a lifetime and requires a totally different kind of care. Therefore, be careful in your choices and make decisions that will keep you strong enough go on to the *Second Baseman, a.k.a., "Humpty Dumpty."*

3ʳᴰ INNING

*"Humpty Dumpty sat on the wall
Humpty Dumpty had a great fall
All the king's horses and all the king's men
Couldn't put Humpty together again."*

If you're familiar with this timeless nursery rhyme, you remember how Humpty Dumpty was shattered into thousands of pieces after falling from a wall and crashing suddenly to the ground, and despite the efforts from all the king's helpers, no one could put ole Humpty together again. However, in this metaphor, Humpty Dumpty can't/won't remain shattered. Instead, like the Bionic Woman, Humpty will/must be rebuilt: "Better, stronger, and faster."

In the game of baseball the second baseman is in a unique position on the field. Because he sits in the middle of the infield (where first, second, and third bases are located) he has a great view of the game as it unfolds. From this position he can see how a player is able to find a way to get on base and advance to first.

He can also gauge momentum and keep you from advancing too quickly around the bases, thereby letting you know you're still only halfway home with more bases in front of you to cover.

In the relationship game, the *second baseman*, **a.k.a.,** *Humpty Dumpty*, sees you as transparent. His location in the middle of the infield allows him to be an observer; and as an observer he has insight into your development in *The Game*. For instance, he can tell you things about the momentum you used to get to first: whether or not you ran full steam ahead or trotted, whether you overextended yourself during the pitches and seemed desperate to hit any/every ball thrown your way, or whether you were a patient meticulous batter that waited patiently for what seemed to be the perfect pitch. In other words, *Humpty Dumpty* is not a *first baseman* and has more time/experience in *The Game*. Because of this, he's able to use these things to his advantage when interacting with you. However, his presence should help you reflect on the lessons you learned after advancing from first.

By the time you reach second base, you should be able to reflect on things such as: While at first, did you choose a guy based simply on the way he looked and his athletic build? You know the one I'm talking about…the guy with the dazzling smile, broad shoulders, and slim, athletic build. The one that never seemed to get that reading/writing thing under control, but could beat up the sun whenever he felt it was shining too much—the one that was viewed by most people (including your close family/friends) as being dumb as a bag of rocks, but you were determined you could *change/save* him. Did you choose that guy that loved himself so much that he anointed you president of his fan club and decided to let you hang around until something better came along? Or did you choose someone with substance... the guy who was comfortable letting you see multiple sides of his personality (including his laughter/tears) and had no problem following directions, respecting others, and was willing to legally put in the work/time to create or get a job? Did you choose someone who had a plan he was comfortable sharing with you and was actually working toward bringing it to fruition without selling his soul/values to do it? Ask yourself if you are the kind of woman that seems to get caught up in whether he's built a certain way, with a certain look, with a certain craving for how trendy he dresses? Or were you able to handle his kindness toward you without coming to see that as a weakness that lacked the *thug* effect you equated with being a *REAL MAN*?

You taking the time to reflect upon these things is crucial because you're supposed to grow with each base and learn which ways to improve on your decision- making, as well as get better at figuring out who you are in the process.

As an integral player in your game, it is the *second baseman's* uses his keen eye of your strengths/ weaknesses that will play a vital role in him beginning the monumental task of putting you back together.

However, just like the *first baseman, the second baseman* has 4 crucial jobs he must perform effortlessly in order to keep you on track and maneuvering around the bases to stay in *The Game.* Again, these jobs may come across as mean-spirited, but they are merely realities that should be viewed as drills that you must master in your training.

The *second baseman's* four jobs are: first, he has to put you back together by rebuilding your trust in men and your idea of being in a relationship; second, he has to be a major supporter in helping you grow intellectually and stay focused to manifest your dreams/aspirations; third, he has to help you learn more things about your sexuality; and fourth, unfortunately, he too has to break your heart.

REBUILDING YOUR TRUST

*Note: Some of you are sitting there reading this have
become angry and quite upset that your heart has
to be broken—not just once, but twice! You fail to
see the relevance of such a harsh reality, but the
same way I emphatically supported its relevance
during your first baseman stage, is the same way I
emphatically support it now. Remember: Daddy
loves you, and this book was not written because I
hate women...this book was written because of my
love for women. Therefore, as tough as it may seem,
there is a reason for the madness, so stay with me
and I will get you where you need to be to see why
your pain will ultimately play a role in your
success.*

After leaving first base, you're in a different place
mentally, physically, and emotionally. If you never took
the time to reflect on your trials and tribulations (as I
suggested you do), you are generally immediately
tagged "Out!" before your feet are planted safely on
second. This occurs because you weren't ready to be
rebuilt and thought you could steal a base and get
away with it. And even if you did make it to second
safely, you would stay stuck there and never know the
feeling of being able to head to third and finally see
yourself in a position to score and make it safely to
home plate. However, if you took the time to reflect (as
I recommended) and learned from your heartache,

you are now ready to receive the *second baseman* and all that comes with him.

When you initially encounter him, you will be cautious and still carrying pain from your disappointing first relationship. Not to worry; because of his job, a solid *second baseman* will not only be able to handle it, he will expect it.

He will be patient and valiant in going about helping you cope with the pain you're carrying from first base. A well-trained *second baseman* has been groomed and has in his arsenal the tools of patience and effective communication. He will use the tools he's been given (just like the king's men in the Humpty Dumpty nursery rhyme) to "put you back together again" and reestablish your trust. You'll begin to recognize him by hearing him say things such as, "All men aren't bad; you can trust me," and "If you were my lady, you would never have to worry about me doing that to you." Although these are comforting affirmations (and in his mind, he generally believes this), the reality is he's also a player in *The Game* and is really only playing his position the way he's innately trained to play it.

SPOTTING THE SECOND BASEMAN

Before continuing to lay out the core jobs of the *second baseman*, I guess at this point it's important for me to help you begin to identify what a *second baseman* looks and behaves like. You'll know him because after your long hibernation, he'll be the one that begins to get you out of the house. He'll be more established financially in his lifestyle and flexible with his time. Look for him to do small "special" things you always wanted a man to do with you, like take you on dates out of state for weekend getaways and include you in hanging out with his circle of male/female friends. He'll be the one romancing and charming you with his cooking in an effort to show you how some men have their own place and are actually domesticated with real abilities to take care of themselves without a woman mothering them. You'll know him because he'll be the one that *initially* accepts that you have a child from your previous relationship and you're trying to go to school to better yourself. You'll know him because finally (over a period of time) he'll ultimately begin to gain your trust and put a bounce back in your step, stride back in your strut, and a smile back on your face...all will seemingly be right with the world. And when he's completed this required job, ultimately he will have succeeded in putting you back together again. He'll have officially become your "knight in shining armor," just like his position requires him to do.

MENTAL GROWTH

Every baseman you encounter should always take an interest in your development as a person (if you find yourself being drawn to one that doesn't...RUN! He's a rogue baseman who means you no good and will potentially break your spirit). Also, any man you find yourself entering into a serious relationship with (meaning BOTH of you have decided to become serious) needs to demonstrate he knows how to be supportive and appreciative of your goals.

Because second base is generally the base that allows you to really dive into exploring the depths of being with a man mentally/emotionally/spiritually on a full-time basis, your *second baseman* will be one of the first men you encounter (outside of your family) to really help you discover the value of being on a team and having a teammate who prides himself in being there to give you mental/spiritual support. As your first real teammate, he'll be able to cheer for you as well as invest his time/energy/resources into helping you move toward achieving some of your adult goals.

To stimulate your mind, he'll be the one that engages you in dialogue on social trends impacting the community, signs up with you to become active in giving back through some form of charity, takes an interest in what you're reading in order to see you defend your views, challenges your interpretation on an issue and appreciates your ability to defend your stance (in spite of your differences on the issue), and enjoys the exchange of learning about new artists/ things you like to experience while sharing with you those things he enjoys.

If your dream is to be a nail technician or a doctor, he's that person who enjoys listening to you paint the picture of what your shop will look like and how big your practice will be. In essence, your *second baseman* will not only be your first teammate, the ultimate goal is for you to arrive at a point where you learn what it's like for your partner to become a real friend.

LESSON OF SEXUALITY

Although sex may come across as a small deal to some women, the reality is that most men find sex to play a HUGE part in holding their interest. Therefore, a good *second baseman* will help you add some skills to your arsenal that will help empower you in being able to keep your skills sharp and ready when they're needed.

Without wanting to become too explicit, I'll simply point out some things that you should be comfortable with at this point and let you begin to fill in the gaps of gauging where you currently are and where you should ultimately be when it's time to leave this base.

The same way you can't learn algebra without having learned basic addition/subtraction, is the same way you can't become a complete sexual being without having learned to be comfortable with touching yourself and the concept of intimacy. (It's okay, you can stop blushing. We're aware that touching oneself is important and you're not the only one who does it. In fact, I'll let you in on a little secret…WE ALL DO IT! Yes, even that person that makes you say, "Ewww!!" while trying to imagine them doing it does it-and if they don't…perhaps that's the reason they act the way the act). Therefore, a good *second baseman* will help you learn how to expand on many of the basics you learned at first base. For example, at first base you may have learned how to touch and please yourself alone in privacy, but at second base you'll learn how to do the same thing in front of your partner and be comfortable with them doing it with you. At first base you may have learned some basics about receiving and giving oral pleasure; at second you'll learn how to appreciate the eroticism and sensuality of the touch, taste, and smell of your partner and how to lose yourself in the moment. At first, you may have tried multiple positions in the privacy of your room; on second, you may find yourself doing it in places that are more adventurous and daring…like at a rest stop on a road trip, in a public bathroom, up against the washing machine, out on the balcony, in the middle of the football field. Remember, life is an adventure, and if you're planning to be a part of it, you have to be open to living it and pushing yourself to new limits.

Naturally, you want to be safe and exude common sense in your choices of adventure, but you also want to be open to life and having fun. You don't want to get old and look back on life and always wonder "what if."

It would be an awful thing to die, get to the afterlife, and then discover that the Creator created you to have experienced life (and all it had to offer), but you found yourself so caught up in someone else's perception of what **YOUR** life should have been that you never got a chance to actually **LIVE** at all. Instead, you more or less found a way to feel content with merely **EXISTING**.

Therefore, get out there, live life, and stop letting other people hold you back!

BREAKING YOUR HEART

I bet you're sitting there wondering why you have to have your heart broken again, especially by a guy who spent so much time going through the motions of putting you together again! A guy who seemed so caring, so charismatic, had so much going for him and taught you so much about yourself mentally and sexually.

He seemed perfect! Just like what you always thought you wanted. Sure, you had made some mistakes in the past (like dating your *first baseman*, perhaps), but this guy was different…and you had learned from those mistakes. This guy was surely the one you had been waiting for, the one you were *destined* to be with, right? The one you could actually see yourself having babies with and growing old with; he's truly your *soul mate,* right?

WRONG!!

It's because you're thinking like this that proves you're still carrying those grand juvenile ideas and suffering from what I like to call *"Post-Cinderella Stress Disorder."*

PCSD is what occurs when your heart is secretly still carrying feelings that you need someone to come

33

along to save you from the horrors of your loneliness. It happens when you still haven't learned to be comfortable in your own skin and content with learning to love yourself and do things **FOR YOU** without needing someone else there to validate and complete you.

Ladies, it's cute in many ways to say things like: "I want someone who completes me." But the reality is unless you've been able to demonstrate you can be by yourself and still be happy, saying this makes you come across as a needy person who has not learned to love/know yourself and can't function without having someone around to save you.

To a man, that's not being a woman; that's being **a dependent**, and it can get you stuck in between bases and tagged OUT!

PCSD also occurs when you still have the cravings of a romantic fiend and secretly feel the previous prince (the *first baseman*) had simply missed his cue to enter the scene the first time and rescue you from your evil stepsisters and horrid family. However, now he's back (reincarnated in the form of the *second baseman*) and ready to claim his bride so finally you two are able to live "Happily Ever After."

It's because you're still thinking like this and trying to shake the ills of Cinderella's powerful telepathic lock (and unaware you're suffering from PCSD) that the *second baseman* as well must play his part in helping continue to move you beyond your fictitious thinking by fulfilling his duty and breaking your heart.

Like the *first baseman*, he too must be careful to do it in such a way that he causes pain, but the woman's spirit remains intact and strong because if he does it the wrong way, the woman will be tagged out and not be able to move on to the next base. In fact, she may find herself becoming bitter and start saying things like, "Men ain't shit and I'm through with their trifling asses."

And the moment these words begin to form on a woman's lips, she has begun to enter the foul *self-doubt zone*, which is a place that (if not corrected early) begins to lead to a broken spirit (which I've already stressed has become a dangerous *no-return zone* for numerous women throughout the free world.)

REFLECTION

After getting your heart broken the second time, you should again take the time to reflect. However, during this reflection, be sure to begin looking at **YOURSELF** and asking yourself what seems to be the issue with **YOU**. (**Note:** We all have issues...yes, even you.) and if your answer is, "It's never me, I'm perfect. It's always the man's fault," you're in denial and having a hard time admitting you too have things you have to work on to grow. This also means you're back in a state of delusion (which, as I previously discussed, requires mental treatment) and you will not be moving on to the next base until you learn to see the errors in **YOUR** actions as well as others'.

At this time, look for patterns in your selection of men. Do they all consistently have the same personality with a different face? And if so, are you getting the same results? If you continuously get the same results from constantly attracting the same kind of men, maybe you should consider acknowledging you're swinging at bad pitches and try changing your approach to *The Game*. And if you found you have tried changing your approach and you still got the same result, ask yourself if your choices got better or worse. If they got better, you're on the right track. You just have to continue to play *The Game* and let it evolve naturally. If they got worse, you need to get back to having patience and not lowering your standards simply because it's not happening in your timeframe. It's a game for a reason, and the game has nine innings that will be played out one way or another, so trying to rush them and skip over them will not only get you thrown out of *The Game*, it will get you put off the team.

In the game of baseball, you must learn that patience, change, and timing are all natural parts of getting what you ultimately seek: a chance to make it safely around the bases and score.

Again, ladies this is all a part of the process of having longevity in *The Game*. You have to learn how to see errors in yourself, your thinking, and your approach to *The Game* so you can grow from them. Therefore, if your *first and second basemen* looked the exact same, had the exact same outlook on life, interacted the same with you, and you got the same end result, is it really necessary for me to tell you that you're a major part of the issue?!

BREAKING YOUR HEART

The *second baseman's* heartbreak is slightly different from the *first baseman's*, but it still must fulfill the desired outcome of growth and reflection. His process might involve asking for his key back or deciding to move out of the place you share. It might require him being direct and telling you he just doesn't see the relationship going anywhere, or your dreams and aspirations simply no longer match his. He might also arrive at telling you he's moving away to take advantage of an opportunity somewhere else and he simply doesn't want to have you away from your family and friends depending on him, because he

37

"doesn't know how long he'll be there and what his next move might be." Whatever it may be, know that this too is part of the natural order and he is also fulfilling his job of helping you prepare to move on to the next base and the *Third Baseman*, **a.k.a.**, *"The Teacher."*

4ᵀᴴ INNING

By the time you reach third base you should be a completely different person mentally and emotionally. Your mindset should have shifted and no longer be operating under Ms. Cinderella's spell. In fact, any and all signs of PCSD should have dissipated by now. This is also the time when your philosophy should begin to center around accepting the concept that people generally come into your life for **a reason, a season,** or **a lifetime.** Therefore, **every man you meet is not meant to be your husband or even a serious candidate.** This epiphany should be taking form in your subconscious and you should now also be open to accepting the fact that, sometimes, they are merely there to help prepare you for where you are ultimately looking to be: at home plate.

Upon arriving at third, you should be in a place/ space emotionally where you're able to demonstrate your ability to roll with the ups/downs that come with relationships and not feel totally broken when things don't work out the way you planned. You should now realize that just because things didn't work out with the previous basemen doesn't mean either of you were bad people (unless your choices were clearly, in fact, BAD and you barely escaped with your life in tact... which means hopefully by now you've reflected on the mistakes of choosing that kind of man and you've grown from the experience); it just means that there is a process in *The Game* and you have to be willing to go through that process to become the best player you can be. And because you are now able to demonstrate maturity in your approach to running the bases, you are now ready to encounter and truly experience *The Teacher.*

Note: Right now you are probably thinking, "What the hell else is there for me to learn? I've had my heart broken twice; I've had my dreams of hitting a homerun my first try at bat destroyed; I've been built back up/charmed only to have my heart broken again! And this arrogant pompous *&^%\$ author has the audacity to tell me I still have more to learn!!"

And my answer to that is, "Yes." You still have plenty to learn, but this time the lessons should not be as difficult because now you've got the maturity you needed to have in order to receive these valuable lessons. There's a valid reason why the *third baseman* is called *The Teacher*, and the only way he can perform his job accurately is if you arrive at this base having shown mastery of receiving the lessons you were picking up along the way as you advanced from first to second and second to third. Although it is true that you have been in the process of learning the entire time you've been in *The Game*, *The Teacher's* job requires special skills that are acquired from years of training (and to be quite frank, although the two previously discussed basemen are in fact integral players in *The Game*, they simply do not have the playing time/skills in the game to offer you what *The Teacher* does).

IDENTIFYING THE TEACHER

With all that being said, this is a good time to give you clues on what to look for when trying to identify what a *third baseman* looks/behaves like. *Third basemen* are veteran players so they have been in *The Game* for a while. They come equipped with things like good credit, 401k plans, property ownership, and are established proprietors/ entrepreneurs, journeymen, skilled tradesmen, tenured at their job (mixed with fancy titles), and have advanced college degrees.

You can generally spot them by their confidence, their ability to come across as truly being comfortable in their own skin, and their content attitude with the choices they've made in life. They tend to have something you can't really put your finger on, but it makes them stand out amongst men who don't have the same trait. Therefore, to put it plain and simple: *Third basemen* flat out have *swagger*. They are sure of themselves and authoritative when they speak. They are polished in their lifestyle, in tune and balanced with their spiritual side, and have become quite comfortable living their lives according to their fraternal motto: "Working hard in order to play hard."

When you encounter him, you will innately pick up on the fact that he's someone that can "teach" you something. You'll find yourself being intrigued by his diversity along with his ability to talk with people on multiple levels. He'll literally have the ability to go from talking with a homeless vagabond in one instance to commanding the attention of corporate CEOs/VIPs the next.

When you converse with him, don't be surprised to find yourself wanting to broaden your horizons and read more. This is because he's well-rounded in his interests and he's able to have insightful dialogue on a plethora of topics that may include spirituality, literature, business, finance, cooking, health care, how to raise kids in today's society, politics, culture, sports, and more. However, do not worry. The way you'll be drawn to him is natural, and it's all a part of his *third baseman* charm/mystique. He's been trained to have an opinion about the world and has worked diligently to carve his niche in it. Also, generally speaking, the *third baseman* is often an older man (at least 5 – 10 years older than you) or a young man (right about your age or a little older with an "old spirit" that's very mature and he has worked relentlessly to get to where he is in his life/career). Regardless, young or old, the *third baseman* is not to be taken lightly and can quickly spot you coming before your feet are firmly dug in and you're ready to advance from second.

Like the previous basemen, *The Teacher* also has three distinct jobs he must perform, but you should be pleased to learn these lessons shouldn't hurt as badly. Remember: Home plate is in your sight and just ninety feet away; all you have to do is stay focused, be patient, remember to apply the skills you've picked up to get here, and you'll be just fine. Unfortunately, a lot of women get tagged out between first and second simply because they fail to make the required adjustments in a timely manner, so the fact that you've actually made it to third base is an accomplishment in itself.

Because of his sagacity, the *third baseman's* jobs center primarily on fine-tuning what you've already learned and helping you prepare to make your final dash to *home*. Again, all this must be done by taking heed not to break your spirit, but it must be done.

The Teacher's three jobs are: First, he must teach you the in-depth psychology of men—what we like, what we don't like, what is seen as acceptable behavior from women to promote longevity/prosperity with men, and what is seen as unhealthy behavior that promotes chaos that will end your relationship before it gets started. Second, his job is to help you master the art/power of seduction and knowing when/how to stroke the male ego. Last, like the others, he too, must break your heart.

Note: I know, ladies at this point, you've probably thrown the book across the room and began scavenging the back cover, looking for my contact information so you can personally tell me how you feel about me, my book, my momma, and everything else that comes with me…but I promise you: If you stay with me, I'll get you where you need to be. Like I mentioned earlier, there's a reason for everything in The Game, but just so you feel better and stop feeling the need to label my book as "evil" and burn it at the stake, if you've been an astute student of The Game and paid close attention to what I've advised you to do thus far, this heartbreak should be the last one you encounter in The Game and it will be a key ingredient in opening doors for you during your next stage. (I use the word "should" here with confidence, but in life nothing is ever a guarantee so I want to leave room for extenuating

*circumstances. However, I'll place high odds on
things being much better from here on in (if you
continue to stay true) than they've been before.
There, I said it. I hope that makes you feel better.*

MALE PSYCHOLOGY

When it comes to understanding male
psychology, unfortunately, a lot of women feel they
learned all they needed to know about the male
psyche when they discovered (during adolescence) the
seductive power of having a *big butt, a cute face,* and *a
nice body.* These women seem to think because they
can get men to notice them when they walk into a
room that they are operating with a magic wand that
will render men mentally unable to think logically and
continue to add up their total value (which, as I
already mentioned, during the detoxification of the
Cinderella Phase, men have no problem doing). Some
women seem to think men are primitive simple
creatures that operate primarily on hormones and stiff
erections.

This analysis might be true for a large number of
young males (11 - 22), but when it comes to dealing
with *third basemen* (who are clearly **GROWN MEN**),
this couldn't be further from the truth. Therefore, if
you're planning to stay in *The Game* to win, my advice
is you learn QUICKLY that there's a HUGE difference

between a **MALE** and a **MAN** (**males** are people born with penises; a **man**: is someone who consistently demonstrates behavior that shows a willingness to accept responsibility for his actions, has a plan and a course of execution for his life, has no problem working hard for the things he wants, and openly embraces and protects his values and the people he loves).

Note: When I use the term "GROWN," I'm not referring to an age; I'm referring to a behavior. Too many times adulthood is based on a number, and with that number comes an assumption that people have had the experiences/time to acquire the ideal levels of maturity. However, as you may have seen (or will one day see) from your dating experiences, every MALE over the age of 21 does not behave at a level of maturity to be called a GROWN MAN (nor has every female over the age of 21 hit a level of maturity in her actions/thinking to be qualified to be called a GROWN WOMAN). This is why you gaining experience/maturity by experiencing each of your basemen is so relevant. Therefore, you should not make the mistake of wasting your time/ energy (like a number of women have been known to do) trying to raise a MALE you have an interest in to become/behave like a GROWN MAN. The sooner you get beyond using age to identify your expectations of GROWN behavior, is the sooner you move closer to being able to have appropriate expectations of the men you have in your life.

LESSONS

Because there's a wide spectrum of lessons that will come from your interaction with *The Teacher*, trying to cover them all will be too time-consuming. However, since there are six crucial areas of concern that could break or make your longevity with a man, I think it's vital to cover these areas so you can get a real glimpse of how analytical men can be when processing your value to the team. These six areas are: intelligence, cooking, cleanliness, sex, maintaining your health/body/image, being confident and maintaining a life of your own, and becoming that which you seek.

IQ

I'm not sure when/where this began or how/why it seems to be viewed by some women as being cute and acceptable, but for some strange reason there are a number of women in the free agency market that seem to believe it's okay to come across as cute, ditzy, and dense. Unfortunately, many of these women still subscribe to an antiquated male doctrine that states: Having a cute face, nice body, big butt, and knowing when/how to be seen/not heard is all you need to get a good man.

*Note: I won't sit here and say there are not a number of
males (as I already defined) who still honor this
doctrine and look to project it on (certain) women
they recruit for their team. However, the women
that males tend to accept "cute, ditzy, and dense"
behavior from are women that are generally placed
on their practice squad. Very few are kept around
longer than a season and out of the ones that are
kept around longer than a season, very few of them
ever make it to being promoted to the starting line-
up.*

Since my purpose in writing this book is to help
the women I love get to a place/space where they
begin to see the importance of knowing how to make
sound decisions regarding the caliber of men they
choose to let in their life, if you are the kind of woman
who prides herself on being this way and would
actually consider being with this kind of man, I think
it's best to ask you why you would want a man who
sees no value in you having intelligence, and how long
do you think you'll be able to hold his attention?

The truth is, a cute face, great body, and big butt
can be GREAT FUN in the bedroom and in public
places where you can be placed on display like a
prized trophy. But the reality is after he's done having
his fun with you in bedroom and there's no one else
around to show you off to, eventually he's going to
want to talk to someone. And if you've positioned
yourself to be his cute dumb sidekick who has as

much depth in your personality/intellect as a Dixie cup of water, it really shouldn't shock you when you find out the person he goes to when he wants a real meaningful conversation…is not you.

As I stated earlier, men will accept certain behavior from women when they have no plans on taking them seriously as candidates for their team. But the moment a man decides he's looking for serious candidates to become his full-time *starter,* you better believe intelligence is at the top of the list.

TESTING YOUR IQ

Ladies, don't be surprised to know men have a variety of ways of gauging your IQ (as I've consistently stated, we're very analytical in our thinking and oftentimes have a method/reason to our madness). One of the common strategies a man will use to begin gauging your intellect is simple conversation. But please know that when he's engaging you in certain kinds of conversations, it's anything but SIMPLE. The conversation might center on things such as: politics, global issues, health care, your thoughts on spirituality vs. organized religion, and a variety of other topics that help show you're well-rounded as an adult and that you come to the team with some depth/diversity. When a man does this, he's demonstrating he's paying real attention to you and actually sizing you up to see if you two will make good teammates. However, if you never get to this level of conversation, there's a high probability he simply doesn't see you as a serious candidate.

IQ/Babies

Grown men (as I've already defined them) recognize women are generally the primary caregivers for children when they're born, as well as the child's first teacher—which means a man also recognizes that when he's looking for a teammate and the woman he's scouting prides herself on being *dumb as a box of rocks*, seems to have only mastered being *cute/ditzy*, lacks depth, only reads love/romance novels, and gets her current events from the *National Enquirer*, his child's chances of getting what he/she needs during the early developmental years are off to a *rocky start* (no pun intended). If you're the kind of woman that takes pride in being this way, get prepared to find yourself being traded from team to team and not taken seriously as a real player.

IQ Games

Just to give you more insight on how strategic men can be, here's some insight on another tool men might employ to assess your IQ: the classic board game *Scrabble*. If you've never heard of it, the key to the game is to randomly pull seven tiles from a bag and spell words based from the letters you've pulled. There is definitely some strategy in how you place your letters on the board to maximize on your points per word. However, the premise is the bigger the word you put down, the higher the amount of points you will gain per word. The game ends when all the letters in the bag have been placed on the board as correctly spelled words and the person with the highest accumulated points wins.

Although this game is good for having fun, talking, and laughing, please know it's also great for helping a person gauge whether or not you're an avid reader. Therefore, if you find yourself playing this game and the only words you seem to come up with are words like: "*the, is, cat, dog, spot, ran,*" and "*no,*" don't be surprised when you find yourself placed on the practice squad with no promises for you to return the next season.

As I said, there's a method to all that men do and when they're in the *scouting phase* of their life, they're paying very close attention to what kind of players they are scouting to be on their team. So when you find yourself being asked a variety of questions about your views, please know it's imperative to your placement on the team and he's checking to see if you've taken the time to invest in yourself beyond being content with having a *cute face*, *nice body*, and *a big butt*. Not having a well-informed opinion about the world as a child is acceptable; not having a well-informed opinion about the world as an adult can get you labeled as immature and not taken seriously as a teammate.

COOKING

The *third baseman* knows you come to the base with a number of misconceptions about the male psyche, so he uses his years in *The Game* to help reshape your thinking on the issue. Through dialogue and interaction, you'll find him testing you to see if you have learned how to take care of your man. (Remember: Males, too, have an instinctive parental side. So even though he's focusing on himself at the moment, don't be surprised to know he's thinking down the road and applying your actions to what they would be like if you two had kids.) He'll do things like show up at your house (with advance notice) to spend a day relaxing with you and wait to see if you have any food in the house and actually take the time to put a real meal together for him. If you fail to see the significance of having food in the house (especially since you knew he was coming over), or why it's a big deal that you don't...you are trying to steal a base and clearly on your way to being tagged out! Again, this is why you coming to understand male psychology is so important.

Initially, he will simply take all the information in and guide you on ways to correct this. Don't be surprised when he begins to offer you pieces of advice on what you should do/have the next time he comes over. *(Note: At this point in The Game, I shouldn't have to mention the timeless cliché: "The key to a man's heart is in his stomach," but if you think this is just some fickle old saying and there's no validity to it, get ready to fail male psychology.)* Men recognize that when/if we are going to have kids with you, the babies must come through YOU. *(Note: Who knows? By the time this book reaches you, maybe technology will have found a way for men to have babies. But if by the time it reaches you, the birthing channel is still flowing through women then YOU simply have to accept this as reality and come to understand why men see YOU being able to cook/prepare a proper meal as significant/relevant.)* Therefore, if YOU don't know how to cook a well-balanced healthy meal for yourself or your man, how the hell are you going to be able to cook and put together a healthy well-balanced meal for your kids when/if they come?! A man feels that if the woman, who births the children, only knows how to feed herself high-cholesterol foods, then when the two of you decide to have kids, not only will he find himself suffering from high cholesterol/high blood pressure, diabetes, and all the other potentially chronic diseases associated with diet (because YOU

are the primary caregiver), the kids will suffer from it
too.

If you operate from a mindset of: "I don't like to
cook; we can eat out" (which is cool every now and
again), or "Why do I have to be the one who's always
cooking?" (which, realistically, you shouldn't always
have to do, but you might want to at least establish
that you have no problem doing it the majority of the
time), you put yourself in a position of having a man
figure you would not be a good caregiver for him or
his kids.

To the naïve woman this may seem frivolous, but
men are strategic, long-range thinkers and they pay
attention to this kind of stuff when adding up your
value to the team.

CLEANLINESS

It has been said that *"cleanliness is next to godliness"*
and from a man's perspective, this is definitely true.
And even though men as a whole have been known to
not necessarily be the most hygienically correct
gender (especially when it comes to maintaining the
day-to-day cleanliness of the house), we do still have a
tendency to hold women to a double standard when
they don't clean. Therefore, don't be surprised to see

men pay attention to how you maintain the cleanliness of your home.

To give you an example of the kind of test some men will give you to examine your overall cleanliness, let us discuss the *Bathroom Test*.

Ladies, when a man comes to your home and asks to use the restroom, sometimes what he's doing is looking to examine your cleanliness. When he's alone in the bathroom, you may be surprised to know he's looking to see how well you clean the throne on which you sit. If he looks at the surface of your toilet seat and it's nice and sparkling clean, this tells him that at least on the surface level you are conscious of your hygiene.

But the inspection does not stop there; next comes *the under-the-seat inspection*. Since most men have been taught to raise the seat when they urinate, this gives a man an opportunity to look for a clean bottom portion of the seat. However, if when he looks under the seat he discovers a microcosmic world of rainbow-colored *Skittles*...this, of course, lets him know you're a surface-level cleaner and raises an eyebrow regarding your overall hygiene.

Now, if you think you've passed the first two parts of the toilet test (because you've been able to clean the surface of the seat as well as the bottom portion of the seat), you're still not out of danger. This is a three-point inspection! The remaining part is when he looks at the side of the toilet. If he looks at the side of your toilet and he can see that you got down all your hands and knees and took the time to completely, meticulously clean all around the screws that mount the toilet to the floor and both sides of your toilet are glistening clean, then congratulations! You have now passed the toilet test! However, if you passed the *seat test*, the *inner bowl test*, and when he looks on the side of your toilet he can see everything you ate last week (and then some) hanging around the sides because you refused to get down on your hands and knees to clean those crucial areas simply because of your laziness or the fact that you thought no one would ever pay any attention to this, it reveals to the man that you are a surface-level cleaner and it calls into question what other parts of your body/home you might be neglecting to thoroughly clean.

This may seem trivial, but as I've been telling you, men are very strategic. What it ultimately tells us is that if you cannot clean your throne well, why should we believe you can do a good job of keeping your *azz* clean beyond the surface level.

I know you've never thought a toilet could tell so much about you, but you've also never been a man.

*Note: Although I only discussed the toilet inspection,
please know that men also pay attention to the tub,
the sink, and other areas of your home. The house
does not have to be spotless, but there are certain
areas that simply act as a reflection of your overall
hygiene.*

SEX

A wise person once said: "Be careful of what you ask for…because you just might get it!"

If you haven't noticed by now, the topic of sex has found a way to be important in every single inning of *The Game*. This was not coincidental. Sex/intimacy is (and always will be) an important part of a healthy relationship. However, when it comes to understanding the male's perspective of how important it really is, you need more insight from *The Teacher*. Simply put: **Not recognizing it's YOUR JOB to sexually satisfy your man can get you put off the team**!

A good sex life obviously varies from *baseman* to *baseman*. The same way no two snowflakes are alike, is the same way no two men are alike. Each one has been trained differently and has come to *The Game* with their individual ideas about sexual gratification. What worked on *first* may not work on *second* and what worked on *second* may not work on *third*. This is why having learned something new about yourself sexually on each base has been pivotal in your development in the game. From here on out, you will need all of your acquired skills to know how to tune in the individual psyche of the current *baseman* you are dealing with and know how to make sure you are giving him what he needs. For example, some men enjoy erotic conversation during intimacy, some like being told how important they are, others like to feel they're in control, some like all of this and more. However, on the other side, some see erotic conversation as too bawdy for their taste, some see being told how important they are as a form of fake build-up and it turns them off, and some would prefer for the woman to be in control in the bedroom. The key is learning to tap into your man's sexual psyche and begin building from there.

Note: I know some of you are sitting there saying to yourself: "What HE NEEDS!? What about what I NEED?!" And to that I say: "Learn to take care of your man so he can take care of you." And if after learning to take care of your man he doesn't take care of you…fire his azz and keep moving! Life is too short to go through all this training only to settle for a baseman who fails to keep himself game-ready. In the major leagues, that can get you placed in free agency, put up for trade, or flat out placed in the pasture for early retirement! I'm not one that believes "what's good for the goose is not good for the gander." Therefore, I can't/won't tell you to have yourself game-ready without also telling you that you have the right to hold your baseman accountable for being where he's supposed to be as well. But as I previously stated, that's another book for another day. In this game, the focus is YOU, so let's stay the course so you can always make sure you know what YOU need to do to have longevity in the game.

A good *third baseman* will teach you to realize that in a long-term relationship, where you have asked (whether directly or implied through your action/behavior) to be the **center** of the man's universe and want all intimate encounters to flow through you, you are also indirectly telling the man that you want to be his everything sexually. By taking on this role, you are telling him you want to be his lover, his *freak*, his *bad girl*, his sense of sexual adventure, and any other thing his sexual psyche decides to tune into. And if your goal as a woman is to have him never look elsewhere, you need to make sure you understand the power you are asking for and know that with that power comes A LOT of responsibility.

From the male's perspective, he's giving you the authority to actually control the fulfillment of his libido for the next several years (if not longer) of his life (and since men tend to peak in their sexual appetites a lot earlier than women, he's often giving it to you in his PRIME). Therefore, not recognizing what you're doing when you fail to maintain the responsibility that comes along with that, or abusing your power by deciding to ration it out as you deem fit...**will get you either fired, placed on injury reserve, or traded**.

From the male's perspective, when you have (and actively seek/desire) that kind of power, he sees you as a person who must learn to multi-task and find balance in playing all the roles of his sexual needs. **Remember:** You asked for them, and now you have to wear the hats! If you opt to become a woman who plays the "I have a headache, my cycle has started, I just don't feel sexy lately, I'm not in the mood" or "If you do this, I'll do that" game every time your man seeks to be intimate with you...don't be surprised when eventually he simply places you on injury reserve and gets someone else to fill that spot to **handle your business** or puts you on the bench and periodically brings you back in *The Game* for relief.

In YOUR mind, this may seem cruel (especially if you're still having flashbacks of that mountain YOU may have placed yourself on in the 2nd Inning and you're back to thinking the world of a two-person relationship is set up to revolve around YOU and YOUR MOODS only), but it's also cruel for you to hurt the team by playing hurt and not taking care of your business. If you are a *player* that's playing to actually make it to home plate and have longevity as someone's wife (or someone's long-term, monogamous girlfriend) you need to remember: "Until death do you part" is a **LOOONNNG** time (hopefully), so if you can't figure out how to keep yourself actively engaged in *The Game* and sexually charged, how long do you expect the *team* to wait for you? No one has an obligation to place their life on hold for you simply because you are into playing power/control games. **Playing these kinds of games will get you sent to the dugout or simply put off the team.**

Note: I'm sure many of you are wondering: "Is it reasonable to ask your man to be considerate of moderate mood changes, as well as recognizing there may be times when you simply aren't in the mood because you're having a bad day?" My answer to this is "Absolutely, yes!" Every player eventually hits a slump or two, but staying in that slump too long (especially when you have been given control of such a large part of a male's existence) will cause alternative solutions to be put in place quickly. Remember: The power is in your hands. If you can't handle it, don't ask for it.

Maintaining Your Image

The best way to begin this conversation is to start with a general observation Albert Einstein made years ago and build from there. According to Einstein's observation, "Women often have a tendency to fall in love with a man's potential and not the man" (I bet you didn't know Einstein was also the Doctor of LOVE)." For example, it's not uncommon to hear a large number of women (when discussing the qualities they are looking for in a man) desire for men to possess the following traits: passionate, goal-oriented, well-built, driven, and focused. From their perspective, these seem to be qualities they initially deem as desirable. But when they meet a man who actually possesses these qualities, unfortunately, these same traits that were once viewed as positives are now attacked for being negatives when they detract from the woman being able to get the man's full attention when she wants it.

To take this a step further, let's take a look at how a general conversation between a man and woman might unfold surrounding this point. The woman's question/complaint in the conversation might go something like this:

Woman's initial question: "Why do you always seem to be so busy and can't find time for us to hang out more often?""

Man's response: "Because I'm **PASSIONATE** about my work and I'm trying to stay focused to achieve my **GOALS**."

Woman's follow-up statement: "Perhaps if you didn't spend so much time working out at the gym, you could have more time for us to do things together."

Man's response: "I definitely want us to spend more time together, but I'm **DRIVEN** to keep myself in decent shape so I can stay **WELL-BUILT** and maintain the image of what attracted you to me. Sorry for being so busy, but I have to stay **FOCUSED**."

Woman's final rebuttal statement: "Well, if you want us to be together, you're going to have to find a way to incorporate me mor into your time and stop acting like you don't have space for me in your life."

On the other hand (continuing Einstein's observation), men have a tendency to fall in love with the image women present to get their attention. Conversely, too many times this occurs without the man having a concrete idea of where the real woman begins and the image ends.

In this observation, both sides have value in their reasoning. However, because they both come from different schools of logic on how they arrived at their needs, these different points of arrival tend to create small to large gaps of ineffective communication within the team.

Note: Since third base is centered on women learning to understand men and the psyche behind our analytical processing, I'll build on this ineffective communication by presenting the scenario from the male's perspective. Since I recognize that no two women are the exactly same, in this example I will focus on those women who are taught that there's nothing wrong with using Cinderella's illusion to their advantage.

If you remember the story, Cinderella showed up at the ball looking absolutely stunning. Everything about her seemed to scream *polished, established, well-off,* and more importantly, *prepared for a healthy relationship.* Yet the reality is it was all an illusion created by her and her fairy godmother to help her stand out in the crowd to catch the prince's eye. To her credit, her plan worked to perfection (which is often the goal for most women when they begin using their charm on a male to get him to focus primarily on her)! The problem, however, begins when Cinderella fails to recognize that the image she presented to get the prince to fall for her is the same image she must now make sure she maintains to keep his attention. And when she begins to no longer have the endurance/ desire to maintain this image, the prince now begins to find himself wondering what happened to his beautiful, seductively charming Cinderella, who has now settled with being content with acting/looking like one of her horrid stepsisters!

DRESSING UP VS. PERPETRATING A FRAUD

Please know there's a HUGE difference between dressing up and flat out perpetrating a fraud: One can get you admired…the other can get you fired!

When you dress up, your true intention is to put on something nice and go out looking your best with what you have. This means you might pull up to the scene wearing the best thing you can afford and sporting it with *light* sprinkles of your own additives/ trimming to put the emphasis on your personal style/ swagger. But as long as you're clean, polished, and confident…you're good to go! The car you arrive in might be a *hooptie* (worn out), but because you're proud to be who you are and comfortable in your own skin, you're able to drive it with your head high and proud to know at least you're not walking or depending on someone else to provide for you.

On the other hand, when you are perpetrating, you go out of your way to be deceitful with the intention of presenting yourself as one thing, all while knowing you're something entirely different. This means that instead of putting on the best outfit you can afford, you go out and borrow your friend's expensive car, jewelry, and clothes so you can appear to have it all together (just like Ms. Cinderella). And the downside to this approach is that when someone meets you under these circumstances, they're not really meeting you...they're meeting a representative of who you aspire to be. Therefore, you are now forced to try to maintain that image.

Sadly, trying to maintain this image now creates a whole new set of issues that could have been avoided if you had only stayed true to yourself.

WHAT YOU SEE IS WHAT YOU GET

It's not uncommon to hear a male come right out and tell a woman, "Based on what you've presented, this person you are right now in this moment/place/ space is the woman I can love for the rest of my life. Whatever you do...don't change."

Not leaving room for a person to change is unrealistic, so there's a lot of naïveté built into this kind of statement. But in all fairness, there are some things that are acceptable as reasonable/realistic/ practical changes that most *basemen* naturally assume come with being in *The Game*. On the other hand, there are other changes that some players bring to *The*

Game without reflecting on how it will impact the chemistry of the team. And in doing so, they fail to realize they are in breach of their contract. Players who have the audacity to commit an intentional breach are harmful to themselves, the spirit of the team, and others around them!

BODY IMAGE

Certain breaches flat out scream for action and can get you traded. Your *third baseman* will help you have a full understanding of why knowing these cardinal rules will save you years of heartache/grief. Let's begin this conversation with body image.

Whereas it's true women come in a lot of different shapes/sizes, it's also true women with those shapes/sizes may all have been able to find the perfect balance in capturing the true essence/personal sex appeal that comes with their body type. The problem begins when women fail to see how by not taking charge of maintaining the particular body type they presented to get admitted into *training camp* (and maybe even ultimately placed in the starting position) is considered to be a **breach of contract** and can become grounds to get put off the team or traded back down to the farm league (no pun intended).

In order to be considered a good player in any sport you must be conscious of the added value that comes with maintaining your overall health/conditioning. This means you must constantly find ways (during your down time) to work out in order to stay strong, healthy, and game-ready. You failing to do so helps demonstrate you have no pride in maintaining your image regarding your health, no cares about your teammate's reliance upon you being game-ready, and absolutely no desire to keep yourself in the spotlight as a valuable player.

Note: Ladies, I'm not writing this with the intention to advocate that you become a hard-body fitness fanatic. However, you thinking it's acceptable to totally let yourself go and blame it all on your metabolism, or making statements about how the 80 extra pounds you picked up without having earned the right to gain weight (that's right, I said it: "EARNED THE RIGHT!") is really no big deal, or you somehow developed a serious "health issue" that caused the weight gain, or you flat out failing to accept your inability to show some self-discipline toward maintaining the image you initially presented will get you placed on the inactive roster and earn you a spot on injury reserve (you can stay inactive for a little while, but staying there too long can get you traded).

For example, if you joined the team at 5'3", weighing 135lbs, and presented an image of you enjoying being active and working out at the gym 2-3 times a week, it's up to you to do all you can to maintain this image. The mere fact that you were spotted in free agency, invited to camp, placed on the roster, and offered the starting position tells you that the image/weight/size you had when you signed up on *the team* is something the team saw as valuable/ acceptable. It should also tell you that *the team* has come to accept this image as a part of your regimen for conditioning and it expects you to either maintain it or increase its intensity.

On the other hand, if you came on *the team* at 5'3", weighing 135lbs, and six months after securing your spot, you go from 135lbs up to 180lbs (without having EARNED THE RIGHT to gain weight—that's right, I said it again and I will continue to say it: "EARN! EARN! EARN!")...then there's a problem and you're screaming to be traded. *(Note: I bet you're sitting there wondering again: "What about the man having to maintain his image?" And to that I say again: "Let's stay focused on YOU; his time will come.")*

Some men absolutely love big beautiful women, so it's not like you can't join a team that has an appreciation for your size and all that comes with it. The key is being able to recognize that when you join a team, whatever image you presented when you initially signed the contract is the same image you have to maintain.

Since some teams like to recruit you at 5'9",
weighing 185lbs, they are showing you from the very
beginning they have an appreciation for your size/
weight and like that you come to *the team* as a *power
hitter*. Therefore, if somehow you take it upon yourself
to go from being a *power hitter* at 5'9", weighing
185lbs, and drop down 60lbs to become a lean clean
125lbs by damn near starving yourself to death on a
celebrity diet where you've been living off spit/water/
grass, you will have just changed your image and gone
from being a power hitter to being a *featherweight,
groundball, keep-it-in-the infield slugger*. And because
that's not what initially got you placed in the starting
line-up of the team, you may now (especially if having
a woman with size is what the man preferred when he
met you) see yourself on the trading block. Again, the
trick to success is knowing what team you're on and
being conscious of maintaining the image that got you
there.

EARNING THE RIGHT

It's now time to deal with the issue you've been
pondering since you first read the phrase "EARN THE
RIGHT TO GAIN WEIGHT." I bet when you read it
the first thing that shot through your mind was: "FS#
% You!" Not a problem; that's a natural reaction.
Especially when more than likely you have never had

anyone be so bold to come right out and tell you this instead of merely thinking it and simply deciding to instantly cross you off of the serious candidate list (despite your efforts to use your Cinderella lure to catch his attention). But since your thoughts of saying "FS#% You" don't change the reality of men thinking this way…**it is what it is and you simply have to woman up and deal with it.**

Me making such a statement is not done for special effect. I mentioned it several times because I want women to understand how crucial this is to the natural process of building a healthy relationship. As I stated earlier, it is naïve to believe there won't be any physical changes that ever occur in a healthy long-term (four-plus years) relationship. In the real world, people age and natural genetic things occur such as: hair loss, gravitational pull (this means *sagging body parts* for those of you who aren't scientifically inclined), and oftentimes there's some minor weight gain/loss. However, the point where this gets crucial begins when it occurs without any natural process or EARNED RIGHT!

Sadly, there are a number of *players* out there who have not earned the right to gain weight and they've begin to flood the *free agency market* with large numbers of obese/out-of-shape players, thus having a huge negative impact on *The Game.*

Many of them have made the crucial error of assuming the natural tightness that comes with a youthful body (ages 17-22) will stay with them deep into their adult years. Some of them actually think because they had natural curves and well-proportioned figures at 19 (without ever having done so much as a sit-up to EARN IT), they're going to be able to go on maintaining their body with the same lackadaisical attitude well into their adult years. They fail to see that the youthful elasticity of their young years will maintain its *snap-back effect* well into their adult years if they've been maintaining it through some form of active healthy living.

However, if they relied solely on their youthful natural figures and never established an ongoing maintenance routine, then when their bodies begin to feel the effects of aging, having babies, and the earth's gravitational pull…they won't have any *"snap back"* to be *"snapped back"* because the youthful warrantee will have expired and the natural elasticity of their muscles will have faded over time due to lack of regular physical activity. And where there's no *"snap back,"* there's trouble!

To be frank, if you haven't had any kids or you don't have any serious health issues that have caused you to gain an unhealthy amount of weight, as far as men are concerned, you have not EARNED THE RIGHT TO GAIN WEIGHT! Therefore, if you're coming to the relationship with no children and already you're 50 to 80lbs overweight (and have no elasticity in place to help return you to your days of glory before the future pregnancy), then more than likely after you have that child you're going to find yourself potentially getting pressure from *the team* to deal with your weight gain and its impact on not being able to maintain your image.

Ladies, please be aware that men recognize babies must come through you. Therefore, most men (if they're sensitive and have common sense) understand that when a woman gets pregnant she's going to have some type of natural weight gain: Her hips are going to spread, her breast are going to stretch and get bigger, and she'll gain a lot of water weight in different parts of her body. All of this is just a part of the natural process that comes with having the responsibility of being the child-bearer. Also, most men understand that after a woman has given birth (depending on her lifestyle before getting pregnant) she will lose most of that weight and her body will begin to apply the *"snap-back effect"* to help her return to her original form before the pregnancy.

In some cases, she may not return fully to her previous form. However, if she had a healthy lifestyle before she got pregnant, practiced being an actively engaged person in a number of activities, worked out on a regular basis, and seemed to have really taken some pride in maintaining her health, then the elasticity of her body will cause the stretches that occur during pregnancy to *"snap back"* toward its original frame.

On the other hand, if she had no *"snap back"* in her form (because she failed to work out and take any pride in trying to maintain any kind of healthy lifestyle), then her body may begin to take on a whole new look/size/structure. Unfortunately, this result oftentimes leads to a woman beginning to feel insecure/uncomfortable with her size, as well as sometimes uncertain about the future of her relationship. So in order to cut back on having to deal with this kind of situation, it is important for ALL PLAYERS (yes, this applies to men as well) to maintain control over the factors surrounding their image as much as possible. These factors all contribute to demonstrating you have EARNED THE RIGHT (there's that phrase again) to gain weight and have body changes.

Note: This may sound cruel, but I'm only pointing out the realities of how a large portion of men think (notice I didn't say ALL MEN, but please believe enough of the men you're more than likely to encounter in your journey will think this way than

*men you'll encounter that don't). The truth
sometimes hurts, but if I didn't care enough to want
to see you empowered to have a better
understanding of your process in developing into a
true well-rounded team player, I would simply let
you continue to walk your path uninformed and
oblivious to understanding what's going on when it
happens to you. And for me, that's simply not an
option.*

BECOME WHAT YOU SEEK

This topic is really self-explanatory. It's common
for young girls to fantasize about growing up and
marrying a man who's financially stable so they won't
have to worry about money and can afford to live a life
of comfort. But if you really want to be with someone
who's been able to find success in whatever field he
has chosen to specialize in (whether they're a doctor,
lawyer, entrepreneur, successful athlete, politician,
scientist, scholar, or realtor), it only makes practical
sense to realize you too have to bring something to the
table. And if your idea of bringing something to the
table is the equivalent of you adding your $14.50 to a
bill that's $14,500, believe me, your time on *the team* (if
you make it that far) is limited.

When you think that kind of behavior is
acceptable, basically what you're saying is: *"Hey
everyone, I didn't really take a lot of time to invest in my
brain or develop any of my personal talents so I could live*

the kind of lifestyle I desire to live on my own. I instead felt it was better to invest in my breast, ass, thighs, hips, and lips so I could be this month's flavor of the month. And if I'm lucky (and really good at stroking a man's ego), maybe I can get him to turn off his logic/analytical side long enough to think with his penis so I might find a way to get pregnant and trap him long enough to have to take care of me for the next 18 years through child support."

By relying only on your body/looks, you're signing an agreement in which the fine print says: "*As long as you can keep this game going and keep my attention (as* the baseman) *diverted from the latest hottest draft picks, you can stay on the team (even if it means you've been reduced from being a serious starter to just being a figurehead that gets to wear a team cap and come out occasionally to wave at the crowd and take team pictures.*"

If that's your plan and that's how you have chosen to approach *The Game,* then your days are pretty much limited and you'll find out very quickly that style of play is not acceptable in the *majors;* that's street ball. And the last time I checked, no street ball player ever made it to the Hall of Fame or got a major long-term deal that offered them security.

Note: This is by NO WAY a personal attack upon the hundreds of thousands of women out there who have become pregnant and found themselves facing the harsh reality of having to raise a child by themselves due to finding out the man they invested their time/energy in (and thought was ready to

*build with them) was simply not a good man and
has gone on to neglect being a father to his child.
This commentary is toward that woman who
intentionally tries to play a game of deception and
finds herself up a creek when the plan backfires.
You can't force people to be with you...even if you
have their child, and the only person that really
loses in this equation is the child.*

On the other hand, when you bring something to
the table, it makes it a lot easier to have an opinion on
what's being served and how *The Game* will continue
to unfold. It's a great feeling to know when you come
to the table, you come as an equal partner that can
hold your own financially whether the male is there or
not. By doing so, you're acknowledging that you're
aware you have options as well, and you don't have to
settle for any *pitch* that's thrown to you simply because
you want to *get on base* and pretend to be a serious
player in *The Game.*

It also makes a relationship run more smoothly
when both people are equally yoked, which means if
your goal is to be in a serious relationship with a
successful person, make sure you have found some
success as well. Who knows? If Cinderella had come
to the prince with more than her great looks and
domestic skills, I'm sure the story might not be held
accountable for creating so many cases of heartache
amongst women.

THE ART OF SEDUCTION

There's an old cliché that says: "It's easier to catch a fly with honey than with vinegar." There are a number of women in *The Game* that fail to see the value in learning the intrinsic art of not only knowing how to seduce a man with honey, but how to do it in such a way that it strokes his ego and allows him to feel that she's truly on board as a player that's totally committed to his well-being.

To take this a step further, some women in *The Game* have not come to understand that when a man is totally turned on by her and she has found the key to mentally tapping into his psyche and unlocking his sexual energy (through knowing when/how to stroke his ego), there are no limits on what roads a man is prepared to travel, no boundaries on how high he will climb, and no obstacle which he will not overcome to show her his commitment to letting the world know she is the light that brightens his world and the center of his universe.

Ladies, if you have never enjoyed history, this is an opportunity for you to study the stories behind some of the greatest inventions ever made, the most spectacular pieces of art ever created, the greatest battles ever fought, and the widest oceans ever crossed (for example, the Trojan War and the Taj Mahal). In doing so, I'm sure you'll be pleasantly surprised to learn many of these things would have never manifested if it had not been for a man's commitment to showing the woman he valued most what he was capable of doing with her by his side and him properly motivated.

By learning to tap into your man's ego, you are showing your ability to go beyond the surface level of just providing him with sexual release. You are showing him your commitment to helping him realize his ability to tap into his inner *Superman*; and when a man has come to discover his inner Superman, you best believe the woman responsible for helping him feel that way will be well taken care of.

Note: Some of you reading this are still on the cusp and struggling with being able to accept what I'm trying to tell you as fact (there are ALWAYS going to be exceptions to the rule, but if 85 % of men are in tune to what I'm saying, then the 15% that are not are a different issue altogether). Some of you want to turn this into a scientific debate filled with a need for documented data from clinical research from fixed/fluctuating test groups and other academic rhetorical analysis on whether or not there is validity to my message. And to those of you that are thinking this way, I say, "Your inability to use common sense, listen to men tell you about men and what we like, and you overanalyzing things to

*a fault is probably why you are still in The Game
trying to make it to home plate. Therefore until you
get that under control, you might not be going
anywhere anytime soon. Sometimes you have to
learn to accept that it simply is what it is and come
to know it as fact.*

By the time you reach *third base* you should be
more than comfortable in your own skin, more than
comfortable with knowing how to please yourself,
more than comfortable with knowing how to tap into
the sexual psyche of the man you're dealing with, and
comfortable with the idea of knowing how to keep
trying new things to keep the sexual excitement fun
and flowing between you and your mate.

Previously I specified how when you ask for
complete power over a man's libido and he makes an
attempt of *trying* to give it completely to you, it is your
responsibility to become completely acclimated with
understanding that with that power comes
responsibility. *(Note: I said trying because if you're not
able to fully handle it right away, he pretty much reserves
the right to pull the plug on that very quickly.)* And by
failing to keep up with that responsibility, you could
find yourself being miserable in your relationship as
adjustments are made to compensate for your
shortcomings.

Consequently, this next discussion will not focus
on the woman who is still struggling to *get with the
program.* This section is for the woman who has been
an astute student during her time of running the
bases, the one who has been a stickler for detail and
worked to get an "A" for every lesson taught, the one
who fully embraces the idea of being the center of her
man's universe and wants to learn how to help him
come to feel he's TRULY found glory. This section is
for the woman that realizes that by helping her man
tap into his ego, she's actually helping him tap into his
inner Superman and pretty much securing his desire
to want to keep her happy. In other words, this section
is for the woman that's ready to embrace the cliché of
knowing *when/how to be a lady in the streets and a freak
in between the sheets.* (**Note:** If the word *"freak"* has
offended you and you feel you could NEVER see
yourself behaving in a capacity that would allow you
to feel comfortable knowing your man is capable of
associating such a vulgar dirty word with you, let
alone your behavior when it comes to sex, **you're too
uptight**, trying to steal a base, and playing in an area
you're TRULY not ready for. My suggestion is you stick
to the base you're currently on and try revisiting this
section when you get over taking yourself so
seriously).

Sadly, to date, a number of women that have been
able to master this level of seduction (in Western

society) are often labeled as *harlots*. However, ladies if
you think about it you'll see there's a reason why these
women are able to keep men coming back for more.
And if your goal is to keep your man from seeking one
himself, you might want to learn more about the
deeper root of her power/charm. In doing so, you'll
come to see that what creates her mystique and allure
is not so much her ability to move a certain way, make
a certain sound, or constantly look a certain way. What
creates her power is her ability to tap into the male's
psyche, feed his ego, and create the illusion of an
atmosphere that fosters raw passion and sensuality.
Therefore, if her ability to do this gets her rewarded
with unlimited marriage proposals, trips to erotic
lands, and his willingness to pay her continuously
even while knowing it's all an illusion...imagine what
it would get you if you're able to do it and actually
have a real sincere interest in loving and being with
him.

That means if, on *second,* you learned to become
comfortable with being more spontaneous and
sexually in tune with yourself as well as your partner,
at *third* you're learning how to multiply that times ten.
In other words, if on *second* you learned how to bake a
two-layer box cake and frost it with icing from the
can, on *third* you're learning how to grow the wheat
that allows you to bake the cake from scratch, churn
the butter using imported cream from exotic places,

and hand-make the frosting from an ancient recipe handed down from the beginning of your ancestral blood line! As always, it's your willingness to let him know you have no problem making him feel kingly that lets him know you're serious about *handling your business* and begins to keep his attention where you desire it to be.

A good *third baseman* will help you realize how making that dirty phone call in the middle of the day (YES, while he's at work) is a great way to help ease tension and keeps him anticipating coming home to finish the conversation *up close and personal.* Taking it a step further, he'll help you see how dropping by the office on his lunch break or meeting for a quick rendezvous can be rewarding for the two of you.

If you're still trying to figure out what to do with that Halloween costume that seemed to command so much attention at last year's ball, look no further! Why not put those handcuffs, that trench coat, those extra high heels, and that garter belt to new use? Believe me, he'll love you for it!

In addition, there's nothing like learning how to reinvent yourself and become someone new. Therefore, why not do role-play? It will shock you to know how far learning to become *Ms. Police Officer, Ms. Secretary, Ms. Librarian, Ms. Naughty Girl, Ms. Boss*

Lady, *Ms. School Teacher*, *Ms. Stranger*, *Ms. Flight Attendant*, *Ms. Doctor*, *Ms. Maid*, or any of the countless other characters you can create will take you. The key is learning to tap into his psyche (without making it obvious that you're doing it or making him feel guilty for wanting you to do it) and letting him know you're more than willing to keep things fun, spontaneous, new, and exciting. By doing this you are creating an atmosphere that fosters raw passion/sensuality that will keep him coveting you.

BREAKING YOUR HEART

At this point you should be comfortable with knowing things happen for a reason and realize that people come in your life for *a reason, a season*, or *a lifetime*. Therefore, seeing a relationship you've been able to learn so much from come to an end should hurt, but it should not break you.

Surprisingly, this relationship is a different kind of departure. Whereas with the previous *basemen* you had to go through the heartbreak to shatter your misconceptions about relationships and the work it takes to have a successful one, this separation is not for that purpose. In fact, this heartbreak is all about *The Teacher* letting you go in order to push you toward *home plate*.

Because the *third baseman* teaches you so much
and comes to the table with so much working in his
favor, it's very easy to see him as your final stop, but
he's not. As *The Teacher,* the *third baseman* is generally
someone that has been around *The Game* for a while
(in rare cases, he may be divorced or separated), so his
veteran status keeps him content with what he's
doing. He's already established that he's good at what
he does and moves with a sense of purpose.
Unfortunately, this purpose is what motivates and
drives him and, consequently, oftentimes keeps him
from making that final commitment to you. However,
his concern and love for you are real. So real that he
knows he can't continue to hold you back from where
you're destined to go and connect with who you're
destined to be with: *home plate*.

As I stated earlier, there's a big difference between
a man that loves a woman enough to let her go so she
can move on to be all she can be *versus* a man that
becomes selfishly possessive and spiteful in order to
hold her back for himself (all while knowing he has no
real plans of ever really being with her). One of the
two is a genuine man who demonstrates he loves her
and only wants the best for her (some may try not to
see it this way due to their emotions getting in the
way), while the other is a selfish male whose foolish
pride unfortunately keeps him from loving her beyond
his ego and, before it's all said and done, would prefer

85

to see her spirit broken before he sees her happy with someone else.

What generally happens when it's time to leave the *third baseman* is what's known as *the congenial separation*. Basically you two arrive at a point where you begin to want him to make the final commitment, but he doesn't and he won't. His reasoning is often that he doesn't want to focus on marriage, but he also doesn't want to hold you back. Please, don't mistake him *teaching* you so much, and the kindred spirit you two share, as you being the one that will change his mind…you won't. Therefore, when you hit this point with him, begin preparing yourself to leave and walk away. Believe me, you're ready for *home plate* and you won't be off-*base* very long (unless you choose to be).

Note: Notice I didn't say "break-up." That's because this separation is not really about teaching a lesson. What makes the third baseman such a special base is the role of being your Teacher on so many levels of your final preparation for home plate; and because the separation is generally congenial, he oftentimes becomes the only one of your basemen you will always have some kind of connection with as a friend and confidant.

Upon completing *third*, you are now ready to turn the final corner and run for *home plate*, where the person that's there to greet you has been waiting

patiently for your arrival. Not to worry; he too has
been an active participant in *The Game* and has been
on his journey, running his own set of bases, and
getting as prepared for you (another book for another
day) as you have been getting for him. His name needs
no introduction and goes back to the days before *The
Game* was a spark in its creator's eye. His name has
two syllables and when pronounced it gives you a
sense of love, comfort, security, pride, and joy (**Note:** If
you've stayed true to *The Game* as I've laid it out, it
should now and always give you these feelings; if it
doesn't, reread this book, identify the problem, and
apply the solution). His name is: *Home Plate,* **a.k.a.,**
Your Husband.

5TH INNING

Before going on to discuss *home plate*, as I'm sure you are more than ready for me to do, I have to take a quick detour to discuss the other players in the game. As I stated in the 1st inning, in the game of baseball there are 9 players on defense and so far we have only discussed those located in the infield. And since not every person that plays *the game of baseball* will hit all the balls pitched to them in a way that will keep them playing *The Game* in the infield (first, second, and third base), I will now address the remaining defensive players.

SHORT-STOP

In every game there's an obstacle that needs to be overcome. Every team that has ever made it to the championship has had its fair share of learning how to overcome the nemesis that seems to keep them from making it to the next level of success year after year after year after year…**and in the relationship game, the biggest obstacle often comes in the form of oneself.**

Believe it or not, it is truly possible for YOU to be your biggest nemesis, not because you are intentionally set on seeing yourself miserable and constantly never moving forward, but because you are hardheaded and refuse to learn from your mistakes and are dead-set on trying to change the rules to a game that was written before you and will continue to be played after you.

My point in bringing this up is to begin moving you toward understanding the value of the *short-stop*. You see, the *short-stop* sits in a peculiar spot on the field (between second and third) and has the ability to almost appear to be a baseman, but the reality is he's not. However, his deception and ability to come across like he is a baseman has caused a lot of women years of unnecessary pain, heartache, and wasted time.

A *short-stop* should be exactly what his name specifies: "a…S H O R T…STOP!" But because so many women seem to feel they can customize their men the same way they customize their purses, cars, homes, and wardrobes by trying to make him something MOST men are naturally not, they have to find out for themselves why this title is so relevant.

The *short-stop* is for the woman who seems to think it's natural to wrap her mind around making any of the following statements and expect to get a different result than what history has shown these kind of men generally produce: *"I like a man who has some thug in him, a man who knows how to check me and keep me in my place"*; *"I want a man who's sensitive and in tune with his feminine side"*; *"I want a man who's about his business and knows how to get out there and get his money by any means necessary"*; *"I want a man that knows how to handle his business in the bedroom, one with a strong back that knows exactly how to work it."*

To the naïve *player*, these blanket statements may come across as having some kind of twisted honor/ virtue associated with them. But to the veteran *players* who have been in *The Game* a while and learned from personal mistakes (as well as from the mistakes of others they have observed dealing with a *short-stop*), they know better.

THUGGISH SHORT-STOP

I guess in a twisted, oxymoronic kind of way, I understand why a woman would want to be with a man that has some *thug* in him. I assume she wants this kind of man because she figures this image brings with it a certain sense of comfort and security against anyone having the guts and audacity to bother her (especially physically). However, the twisted irony that comes along with this kind of man is, oftentimes literally, "HE'S A DAMN THUG!" which means he's someone who has consistently demonstrated his inability to make smart decisions (especially when it comes to his emotional stability/temper when he's upset...hence this being a major contributor to why his *azz* is called a *THUG*).

Therefore, when you get with him and find out his way of dealing with his aggression is kicking your *azz* and whooping up on you when he has run out of other people to intimidate, hopefully you too will have come to realize why he's called a damn *short-stop* and get your mind off of equating safety/security with validating thuggish behavior as being cute/acceptable. And if you still don't get it, give it some time and let's see what *The Game* looks like for you in the next few years. If after a few years you find that you still enjoy getting your *azz* kicked, getting smacked around, intimidated, isolated, and held hostage by your thuggish protector...then keep doing what you're doing.

And if you come to realize you mistook your *short-stop* for a real *baseman,* you've seen the error of your ways, and you're ready to move on, start putting together your plan of escape and begin trying to move on. (**Note:** That's right, I said *"escape"!* I say this because in most normal relationships, you have the option of being able to **break-up** and leave the relationship **on normal terms with normal break-up rules**. However, when it comes to breaking up with a *thug*, your options are pretty much limited to trying to **escape** and hoping he doesn't find out where you're headed before you get there. Again, he's a damn *thug* for a reason...and you trying to use normal logic with him during *the breaking-up phase* is not going to sit well with him.)

THUG VS. WARRIOR

Ladies, I don't want to totally rain on your parade by acting like I don't know what you're looking for when you find yourself being drawn to the alluring traits that many of the *short-stops* seem to exude. But I do want to make sure you know that *short-stops* are those *males* that seem to be on the extreme end of the spectrum and have not been able to find that comfortable medium of knowing when to turn one trait on and an inferior trait off.

For example, I recognize that when you say you want a man with a little *thug* in him, what you're generally saying is that you want a man who has it in him to be dominant when needed, aggressive in certain situations, and protective of you at all times. Where the problem begins in this conversation is the language you've chosen to use to describe what you want; and by failing to express exactly what you want, you have opened yourself up to attracting the wrong kind of masculine energy.

What you actually want is a warrior, not a thug... and believe me, there's a HUGE difference in the two. A warrior is a man who stands for something and has no problem going into battle mode when/if the situation calls for him to do so, but on the other hand he's also able to recognize there's a time to relax and enjoy being at peace. However, a *thug* is really a damn brute that has no on/off switch. His point of existence is centered on intimidation and he takes pride in seeing people be scared of him. There's no valor in why he moves and behaves the way he does; he's simply out of control and eventually will run across someone that will be more of a *thug* than him (or a real warrior) and find himself having bit off more than he could chew.

SENSITIVE SHORT-STOP

Some women, for whatever reason, have decided that they want to be on the opposite end of the *thug* spectrum and prefer their men to be in tune with their sensitive/feminine side. These women feel it's

important for a man to be able to demonstrate he's
comfortable with being able to show sensitivity for
others by being extremely empathetic about the world
and all its pain/suffering. Some even like it when their
man goes so far as shedding tears when they're
overcome with the emotional turmoil of caring so
much for those who have experienced trauma.

Again, I totally understand why (theoretically) a
woman would be attracted to this kind of man. This
kind of man appears to have the ability to understand
the importance of human life, values doing right by
others (sometimes to a fault), and is comfortable
enough in his own skin to know it's perfectly fine for
men to show their partners they have *real* feelings that
are not always stern and that men are in fact capable
of being emotionally invested in matters outside of
themselves.

The problem in this scenario generally occurs
when something tragic happens and you're looking
for the comfort/security of your man to make you feel
protected, but instead you find yourself comforting
him and trying to figure out why he's always crying
more than you! This is where you need to recognize
that you're dealing with a *short-stop* and take a hard
look at the reality the kind of man YOU selected.

Whereas it's great to have a man that's capable of demonstrating love/concern for the world around him, it can become somewhat overwhelming when you come to realize he cares TOO much and it affects his emotions to the point where he's no longer demonstrating traits that are associated with male behavior at all. In fact, he's more or less demonstrating traits that are commonly (in a number of male circles…notice I didn't say "ALL" male circles) associated with pretty much coming across like a b@# S%, a punk, a scrub, a weakling, etc., which is never a good thing to be associated with.

Note: I'm sorry, I tried to think of better words, but sometimes it simply is what it is.

HUSTLER SHORT-STOP

There's nothing wrong with wanting a man who's a hard worker. In fact, being a hard worker is an admirable trait in anyone. The problem that comes with wanting a person who's down for getting his money *by any means necessary* is that it leaves the door open for too many codes of ethics/values to broken in the process. *By any means necessary* generally translates to mean: "No matter what I have to do, who I have to hurt in the process, or how much of my soul I have to sell to get it, I will do it as long as at the end of the day I have made some money." Therefore ladies, in relationship terms, what he's actually saying to you is:

"So what if I made bad decisions in my life and decided to not take investing in myself with a solid education as real, I'm a victim of circumstances and I have the right to feel the world owes me something. Therefore, even though I failed to acquire enough education/patience to create an opportunity for myself legally, I feel justified as long as I can rob other people and make them victims of my lack of preparation. And since life is all about me, you and the world should accept me for me because I'm just keeping it real and staying true to my code of 'excuses' and frivolous bullshit!"

Note: Although I focused primarily on the lower end of the hustler circle, I want to make sure I state that some of the biggest hustlers in the world come with college degrees and pedigree backgrounds (i.e., Bernard Madoff and Jeff Skilling), but if their behavior and mindset is the same (if not worse) as the hustler from the lower end of the spectrum, it's all still the same. Just because he comes dressed up in a pretty package, with a fancy title and new suit doesn't stop him from being what he is—and in the end, the results are the same regardless.

As horrible as that may sound, what he's also saying to you is: *"So what if we have kids that are depending on me and need me to be there every day as their father to help nurture/feed/guide them. As long as I am able to go out and make ends meet by committing crimes to keep a new pair of shoes on my feet, cash in my pocket, and trendy clothes on my back to keep myself feeling like I'm my own man…what difference does it make? You go ahead and keep hold down the fort and taking on ALL the responsibility without me."*

Hopefully you can now see the blatant reality of the image I just painted regarding this kind of male and why he should definitely be a *short-stop*. However, if you've yet to see it, let me take a moment to build more on my point by plainly stating the following truths: This kind of person is really selfish, has an attitude that makes him feel the world owes him something, and unless he comes to accept responsibility **for his actions** and develop some form of values that lets him know all money is not good money and some things you simply have to say "no" to regardless of what the end result may be, he's going to always be a threat to himself and the people around him. So my question to you now becomes: Why put yourself in this position? What kind of *man* intentionally puts himself/loved ones in harm's way by doing wrong to others and has no problem going back/forward to jail simply because he refuses to change? *Answer*: "A *male* who's confused about what manhood is and a *male* that you can't save from himself." Therefore, do yourself a favor and lose the ideal of thinking a *male* that has this kind of attitude will ever turn into being a *man* you can build with.

Note: By NO MEANS will I EVER say a person who may/may not have dropped out of school and works to make an honest living in a non-traditional way through a legitimate hustle is in ANY fashion doing anything wrong. Nor will I ever say they are not

*being stand-up citizens that openly embrace
creating opportunities for themselves in order to
care for their families/responsibilities. However, I
am saying if the shoe fits, wear it! I'm not
apologetic for calling a spade a spade.*

LOVER SHORT-STOP

In the bedroom, his skills are legendary (in his
own mind). He's known in his circle for being a d^&*
slinger/head board banger, an *azz* smacker/toe tapper.
In fact, every time you think of him, all that comes to
mind is the visual of the last time you two were
together and how he made you make sounds you
thought were limited to gospel revival sessions!

Because of his *special skill* set, you've dubbed him
Sir Slang-a-Lot and you refuse to come down from the
cloud he's able to place you on whenever you two
have intimate time. But because you fail to come down
doesn't stop the storm of reality from creeping in and
wreaking real havoc upon your world when you finally
begin to realize that being a great d^S* slinger is ALL
he's really good for! And last time I checked, a *male*
being good in the bedroom doesn't help feed the kids
(unless that's his profession, which is a totally
different conversation), doesn't help pay the rent/
mortgage, and doesn't help show that he's responsible
as a *man*. However, what it does show is that he's
attentive to your body, has stamina, is potentially well

endowed, is in tune with his body, and he's cool with being **a stud**. Therefore, if you're looking to equate him making you feel good physically with him also having the traits to be a great investment for a long-term relationship based solely on his *special skills*, you might want to think again.

Ladies, please know that by no means have I mentioned all of the personalities you will come across that have been dubbed *short-stops*, but this is at least a start for you to begin thinking about the mindset/energy you may be exuding that would attract this kind of male and ask yourself if that's the path you want to continue to follow.

SHORT-STOP CENTRAL

Because there are so many more *short-stop* personalities I have not mentioned, the following is a brief list of other extreme examples you may run into at this position:

Mr. Inconsistency—The guy who always seems to find a way to paint the perfect picture, but never seems to know how to really begin or close the deal. He's the one that never seems to know what happened and why he didn't see what happened coming.

Mr. Momma's Boy (the distant cousin of Mr. Sensitive)—The guy who is grown as hell in age, but has not been able to pull himself away from suckling his mother's breast and become his own man. Although you've been in a relationship with him for quite a while, he still hasn't figured out if he's dating YOU or his mother. In fact, he still calls her every other day to keep her up to speed on every move you two are making, just so he can make sure she approves and doesn't feel left out of the *special* love you and him have for one another.

Mr. Stringalong—The guy that's content living with you and making promises of marriage, but after 3 years has still not found a way to make it happen. Better known as **"The Liar,"** he'll lie like a Devil to make sure his agenda stays in the forefront. He'll lie about the trip he intended to take you on, the car he was planning to buy you, the bills he intended to pay, and the money he had coming. He's so serious about his lies that he'll lie about being upset that you had the audacity to ask him if he was lying!

Mr. Big Baller—The guy who has so much on the go with so many *BIG* deals on the verge of getting ready to happen, knows so many *important* people, has been to so many *important* places, but he can't find time to stop talking about himself to hear what you have to say. In fact, he's so good at what he does that he oftentimes refers to himself in third-person or uses the plural version of himself by saying "*we*." But please know when he says "we" that it does not include "YOU."

Mr. Dreamer (the second cousin of Mr. Big Baller) —He's the guy that has BIG DREAMS and plans to make it BIG, but has never taken the time to finish anything (not even school) and is always talking about what he's going to do when his time comes.

PATHWAY TO SHORT-STOPS

The way *short-stops* generally find a spot in your life is when you fail to make sure you're clear on what you want. The vaguer you are about what you want when you first start dealing with a man, the more you leave room for misinterpretation that could later come back and haunt you. For example, if you started off seeing a guy under the guise of the relationship being simply sexual and somewhere in the process of dealing with him YOU decide to develop feelings that make you feel he's the guy you want to have a serious relationship with, please know that YOUR developing feelings and trying to change the rules to the game does not necessarily mean he has to comply with your changes or vice versa.

A lot of guys have a tendency to be very consistent and compartmentalized when they decide to start adding things to their *line-up*. Therefore, if you joined the team by filling out the BOOTY CALL application and was content with that slot when things started, don't get mad if, when you find yourself catching feelings and wanting to move up to the *starting position,* he stops you dead in your tracks and tells you you've reached your glass ceiling. As painful as this may be, you have to recognize that when there are different spots on the roster and you willingly fill one, **you can't apply for the booty call position and think it holds the same requirements as the wife position!** Believe me, they are two TOTALLY different screening processes. One (at the bare minimum) requires a nice body, a big butt, and a cute smile, and doesn't come with a lot of time/patience requirements; the other requires time, patience, love, and a gaggle of other things that the BOOTY CALL applicant simply was able to forego because of their limited job requirements. Therefore, make sure if you can't handle this aspect of *The Game*, don't put yourself in a position to play it.

In addition, if you should happen to get to a point where you find yourself being with someone who already has someone else, please know you going into this relationship does not automatically give you *starting position rights.* Which means if he has told you he's leaving and he NEVER seems to do it, you're dealing with a *short-stop* and you need to ask yourself how long you want to stay in that situation. **Note:** Don't be surprised I brought this up…it's a part of life and we all know it happens. There are entirely TOO many factors involved in why people tend to get to this point (including many which have been discussed in this book), so I'm not going to pass judgment regarding it being a good or bad thing. However, I will say, "If you're not handling your business, more than likely someone else will."

Again, there's nothing wrong with being drawn to *short-stop* traits, but the reality is you want a man that has been able to find a balance in possessing several of these traits at once, but not on the extreme end of any of them.

6TH INNING

OUTFIELDERS

In every game, there will always be players that are stand-outs. In major league baseball, these are often elite players that drive paraphernalia sales sky-high, keep fans coming back for more, and consistently play at a level that allows them to be rewarded with a nomination to the All-Star game.

The All-Star game is one in which only the current elite players get invited to play, and in rare cases this invitation can become a player's gift as well as their curse. It's a gift because in a game filled with stars, this player has been able to demonstrate they're a star amongst stars. On the other hand, it becomes a curse when the All-Star player begins to believe their own hype and think they're the greatest thing ever to wear the uniform and no one could ever do it better.

In some cases, this player takes their cockiness a step further and begins trying to hold the team hostage by making outrageous demands of what the team has to do if they want to keep them on board as a player.

Much like the game of baseball, in the relationship game, there are always going to be star players that stand out in a crowd, players that come with exceptional talents and make other people feel better about themselves as players and feel completely drawn to them. These are the players that, in many cases, go on to hit *homeruns* (by going on to develop healthy, long-term relationships that are filled with happiness/ success) after their first or second try at bat. (**Note:** As I stated, in "**any game**," there are always exceptions to the rule, so this is not a contradiction of the statements made earlier in the book regarding this being a rare occurrence.)

The problem begins when we start talking about the odds of it happening and combining those odds with the uncanny number of *players* that think they're all-star material, but they're not. Ironically, many of these *wanna-be* All-Stars can't even get invited to sit in the stand as a fan at an All-Star game. Some of these are the women that believe they bring more to the game than what they actually bring and have done a great job of convincing themselves they have the talent to come to a team with high demands.

Unfortunately, many of these women have read too much into their own hype and have come to believe it as the truth. Much like one of the *short-stops*, they've done a great job making themselves **legends in their own mind**.

Since these women are in fact a part of *The Game*, naturally there has to be a position on the field that deals with this kind of thinking. With that being said, because there are so many of these *players* out there, *The Game* comes equipped with three positions that make it their business to keep the balls that are hit by these women from **ever** leaving the ball park and being counted as homeruns. These three players are called *outfielders* (left field, center field, and right field), and they specialize in being able to run down any ball that's hit by the *wanna-be* All-Stars.

In fact, it is the *outfielders'* job to keep giving the *wanna-be* All-Stars an understanding that the *real Game* is being played in the infield on first, second, and third base; therefore, anyone trying to avoid having to cover each one of those bases by attempting to step up to the plate and dictate how *The Game* is going to flow, how the rest of the *players* will behave, what *pitches* will/won't be *pitched*, and when/how *The Game* will end will always get their balls caught in the *outfield* and have them **tagged out** before they can ever get started.

All of this means that if you're woman that lives by any of the following statements, you're playing *The Game* in the *outfield* and more than likely you won't be making anyone's *real* team anytime soon:

"In order to get with me, a man needs to be making at least close to or above six figures."

"I can't see myself being with a man that doesn't drive one of the best-looking cars on the road; I have to look good when I pull up on the scene and last year's version just won't do."

"I'm a born-again virgin; therefore, if a man wants me, he'll be willing to wait for intimacy as long as I want him to or until he puts a ring on my finger."

Note: With this particular statement, I have to take a moment to acknowledge that a number of women get to a place/space in their lives when they make this statement based on finding themselves at a religious crossroad. And because of that I want to take the time to acknowledge that no one has the right to invade or try to stop you from having your spiritual quest of growth with your Creator. If this is where you feel you're at, I wish you the best in your journey and I hope you find what you seek. On the other hand, if you're a woman that's been actively having sex for years and suddenly you decide—for whatever reason, outside of it being a spiritual journey—that you no longer want to engage in physical intimacy, I won't say you don't have that right, but I will say the kind of guy that's generally going to accept this will be someone that's located in the outfield…so get ready for it and let the game begin.

"My man needs to be able to take total care of me. I don't want to work—that's the man's job—and if I have to work… why am I bothering to be with him?"

"A man needs to look like a supermodel and be built like a Greek god before I would even consider giving him the time of day."

Whereas these may seem like extreme statements, I'm sad to announce that these are very real statements and some women actually think it's acceptable/healthy to think like this. **Note:** Notice I said, "You won't be making anyone's *real* team," the key word being *"real."* If you are a woman that thinks you're more than what you are and tend to come with demands that **most men find repulsive/unrealistic,** you might every now and again find a man who's willing to entertain you by acting like he's going to let you actually hit the ball far enough for it to be a real *homerun.* But, believe me, it's all for fun and he's putting on an act!

Generally speaking, *outfielders* like to run and they pride themselves on having the speed to cover a lot of ground, so at the last minute—when you think the ball you hit is getting ready to land in the upper bleachers and the crowd will be brought to its feet as you take your time rounding the bases to celebrate your *game-winning homerun*—they can be there timing their *jump of denial* just right, so as the ball is falling an awaiting open glove will rise like a phoenix from the ash at the last second (along with the *outfielder's* tongue hanging out of his mouth in anticipation of robbing you of your glory), so you will be called "OUT!"

Ladies, these players have resources as well as *game* (meaning they're good at entertaining themselves at your expense), and they take pride in being able to keep sending you back to the dugout to wait for your next turn at bat so they can see if/how you've learned your lesson and regrouped on your strategy for trying to get around the bases.

OVERACHIEVERS

I want to say it's ever a bad thing for a woman to have high standards when choosing a man. In fact, it makes perfectly good sense that she would want to choose someone she sees as being worthy of her attention, admiration, love, and affection. But the problem that seems to come into play with most women that discover they're dealing with *outfielders* is that a large number of these women don't bring **any** of the things they're demanding to the table themselves, yet they think it's perfectly feasible for a man to give two cents of a damn about their demands. (**Note:** If this is describing you, you should revisit the *third baseman* in the 4th Inning and pay special attention to the section on *Becoming That Which You Seek*.)

On the other side of this scenario is the woman that has a lot going for herself, but has unfortunately placed more value on herself than what the *free agency market* has deemed the time/effort of trying to get with her is worth. For example, one version of this is the woman whose expectations of hitting a *homerun* is based on superficial things. She's the one that thinks because she went to a certain school, got a certain degree, has a certain kind of income, drives a certain kind of car, and lives in a certain kind of neighborhood, men should be lined up waiting to grovel at her feet simply because she did what she was supposed to do and put herself in a position to take care of herself.

Again, this is not to say a woman should not hold her head high for her accomplishments and set a standard for what she sees as quality traits in her potential mate. The problems this particular woman seems to keep running into is that she doesn't really allow anyone outside of her limited perception of good pedigree to get close enough to discover she has any real substance. Therefore, she fails to realize the guy she's passing judgment on for not having the image she deems as perfect is the same guy that might have more going for him than she can imagine, is capable of loving her beyond her expectations, and carries more qualities of being a real man in his fingernails than many of the men she's waiting to deal with are carrying in their entire DNA. And because she's so emotionally dense, the outfielder is in place to keep stringing her along and robbing her of her homerun until she begins to see the error of her ways and finds a way to develop some real substance.

JEALOUS DRAMA QUEENS

There are entirely TOO many types of drama queens to address all of the personalities that outfielders are willing to date. Yet, this book would not be complete if I didn't take the time to address the Queen of all drama queens, Ms. Jealousy.

Truthfully speaking, this section is a gray-area because there are a lot of males who like/welcome having a jealous mate. In contrast, there are quite a few men (and males) who want nothing to do with any woman that show signs of having jealous traits. However, since the men who welcome extreme jealous behavior tend to be true game players, it should make perfect sense why I would discuss this as an outfielder's topic.

As I mentioned earlier, outfielders like to entertain themselves at your expense. They see your jealous behavior as something to play with until they grow tired and decide to move on. Yet, on the other hand, if you are dealing with a second or third baseman, they will see your behavior as being too overbearing, too jealous-hearted, and too insecure.

If you're the woman who takes great joy in putting a leash/muzzle on your man to control his every move (because you can't trust him, or you have issues that tie into your lack of self-esteem), there's a high probability that you are dealing with a short stop or an outfielder. Therefore, depending on the severity of your experiences with this issue, try to make a conscious observation of your behavior to insure you have not fallen victim to having a broken spirit.

Don't get me wrong, ladies, sometimes it's cute (in a playful kitten kind of way) to see you become protective of your interest, and to watch you establish that you are the one and only QUEEN of your domain. To be honest, most people like to know that their mate cares enough to become a little feisty every now and again (especially if the mate feels someone is potentially being a threat and receiving more attention from their spouse than they are). However, there's a BIG difference between cute feistiness and lunatic jealousy. For example, cute feistiness sounds like this: "What's that new fragrance you're wearing? It smells great. I'm going to have to keep my eye on you to make sure none of these women are checking you out and trying to steal my man." On the other hand, lunatic jealousy sounds like this: "How come every time you walk out the damn house you have to have on cologne?! I told you, if you are not with me, you are not to EVER wear cologne! I don't want any of these damn females getting any crazy azz ideas!" To some, this example may come across as extreme; but for many, this is their normal way of thinking, and they don't see why I'm making such a big deal out of it.

Ladies, the moment your kitten-like feistiness begins to constantly turn into the tortuous terrorism of a vicious territorial lion (for no reason whatsoever, except for your personal insecurities), then you're setting yourself up for failure. Most mature men are not going to accept this, and will RUN (rightfully so) the hell away from you. No one should have to live their life as a prisoner to someone else's "love." And if controlling your mate's every move is your version of what love is, I suggest you seek professional help to get a better idea of what REAL love looks like. You can't OWN a person and no one has the right to own you. If your mate does wrong by you, you have the right to make a conscious decision to stay or leave, but choosing to stay does not make you their owner.

For those who feel this is irrelevant to you (even though you clearly show signs of being extremely jealous-hearted), for the record: even if you're currently with someone, who seems to welcome your jealous rants, you should begin to look closer to make sure they're not with you merely because you're crazy as hell and they simply have not found a way to ESCAPE! Believe me, being extremely controlling and jealous-hearted is not normal, and most NORMAL people would not stay and put up with it.

Note: If you are the person I have described, the reality is no one, but you, knows all the things you have gone through to get to this point. If your reason for being this way has nothing to do with something someone has done to you, you have to work HARD to overcome this, especially if you're planning to make it to home plate (and stay there). On the other hand, if tragedy has left its impact on you to the point where you can't trust, you should seriously consider getting professional help to confront these demons. It may hurt, and trying to overcome it will not be easy; but if you're planning to be in a well-balanced relationship, eventually you will have to stop allowing this to control you.

EXPAND YOUR HORIZONS

This final area is one that's very hard for me to write, but again, in order for me to stay true, I have to be open and honest with my message. It's hard to live in a country that carries so many "-*isms*" in its history (racism, separatism, sexism, etc.) and continues to struggle with effective strategies for rising above many of its social barriers. But as the game of baseball has shown, star players come in a multitude of ethnicities and from a variety of different regional backgrounds. In fact, it's not uncommon to look at a team and see players from at least five different countries playing on the same team and having found a way to obtain major success in doing so. I bring this up because I want to take a moment to address the issue of race when it comes to choosing *your team*.

As much as I want my daughters to marry a man who looks just like me and shares my racial background/history — **Note:** If you find it surprising I would say this, you shouldn't; I'm just keeping it real and stating the truth of what most fathers feel and want for their baby girls. However, in all honesty, the bottom line is **I want them to be happy first and foremost**.

To be totally honest, I damn sure don't want to ever see my daughters get to a place/space where they see it as acceptable to discriminate against men from their own racial background/history, but I also don't want them to waste their lives waiting for *a man* from their own ethnic background to do right by them when someone from another background has shown the interest/ability to step up to the plate and make them happy. Therefore, if you are that woman that's sitting there reading this and you've tried dating men of your own ethnicity a hundred times over and, at the end of the day, you find yourself still being alone, hurt, and trying to cover *the bases* one way or another…you might want to get it out of your head that it's all about race and try expanding your horizons to include ALL serious candidates instead of wasting away waiting on one limited group.

Ladies, if you've finally slowed down long enough to reflect on your experiences and in that reflection you've come to realize that trying to stay true to the message your parents gave you regarding race while growing up still has not brought you the kind of satisfaction you thought you would/should have, maybe it's time to admit your parents made a mistake by teaching you to limit yourself. Even worse, maybe it's time to realize that until you open yourself up to really GROW, you will continue to find yourself out in the middle of *center field* being tagged out bat after bat after bat. In other words, *life is short. I advise you to get out there and get involved with living in it versus trying to stay true to a jaded principle that has never brought you any substance, satisfaction, or happiness.*

On the other hand, if your pride/stubbornness/ fear of becoming **your own person** keeps you from being able to make that leap…good luck with what you've been doing and I hope it works out for you. **Note:** This is by no means a testimony that one ethnic group is better than another, nor am I promising that by getting with someone outside of your race you're guaranteed to find happiness. This is, however, is a statement that says *if you haven't been able to find happiness by staying true to the racial group you've come to identify with, why not expand your horizons? Who knows? You might actually learn something new and grow as a person. The worst-case scenario is that you come to realize that being a good or bad person is definitely not limited to race.*

7TH INNING
STRETCH

In baseball, the 7th inning is when you normally take a moment to pause from the game and revitalize the spirit of the crowd. This is normally when the crowd joins together to sing that classic ballpark tune: "*Take me out to the ball game…*"

Well, in this *Game,* the 7th inning is when we come to heal and try to understand the mistakes that have truly gone astray and landed you in the *"foul self-doubt zone,"* which eventually put you on the track to having a broken spirit instead of an amendable broken heart. And hopefully by the time you reach the end of this inning, like in the real game of baseball, you'll be rejuvenated and ready to lift your voice to sing in harmony with the crowd: "*Buy me some peanuts and Cracker Jacks…I don't care if I never come back!!*"

BROKEN SPIRIT

Throughout this book, I've referred to how imperative it is for each *baseman* to take the time to do his jobs with care and without malice. You've also seen me warn of what could happen if, when doing his job, he behaves in a cruel, malicious, and spiteful manner that completely negates what the intentional heartbreak is designed to do.

In case you forgot, each time I warned of the damage that could be done if a *baseman* failed to do his job of temporarily breaking a woman's heart and instead made the grave mistake of breaking her spirit.

When a woman's spirit gets broken, she reacts in a variety of ways. Many of these reactions go far beyond what I'm going to address in this book, but I will touch on a number of the reactions that are within grasp of being controllable before they become too extreme and she's completely lost.

Sadly, some women have experienced such bitter pain by the actions of *males* that it's hard for me to imagine the depth of their sorrow and even harder for me to write about it. This pain often runs deep through the woman's core, like hot lava running at the core of a volcano, and it seems to gain momentum day after day. Upon further examination it's often revealed to be a pain that reflects lost innocence and may stem from horrid memories of having experienced childhood abuse, or it's a pain of someone's contorted image of love and may carry the scars from domestic violence. Lastly, it may be the pain from the trauma of an unsolicited sex crime that continues to cast its demons upon its victim. And although a lot of women have been able to find the inner strength, self-love, and support to come through these pains, **there are plenty who have not**.

Because of the sensitivity of this matter, for the sake of staying true with my message, I will touch on the issue of the *broken spirit*, but more specifically my focus will be on women who have had their spirits broken and responded in any of the following ways:

1) opt out of being with men altogether and have decided to take on same-sex relationships; 2) opt out of ever being involved with any male that shares her ethnic origins/history; 3) have decided that instead of being "victims," it's better to become "predators"; 4) have come to the point where they are unable to trust men at all and are very critical of male energy.

SWITCH HITTER

Some people make the argument that sexual orientation is something we're born with and people don't consciously decide which orientation they will gravitate toward. I'm not going to get into that argument and my personal feeling on it is to each their own: "*If you like it, I love it!*" Yet, although my goal is not to be controversial, I will say there are a number of women in *the stands* who were once *players* on the field, and because of getting their spirits shattered by a *rogue baseman* they made a conscious decision to leave the *male Game* and switch to the *female Game*.

Some of these women have convinced themselves that by being with a woman, they're with someone who shares their emotional outlook, nurturing spirit, and gentle touch. Unfortunately, in some cases, these women become extreme in their views of men and vow to live under the creed that "**ALL men are created evil**" and are never to be trusted with their hearts or friendship again. When this creed or mindset is adopted, it becomes interesting when we examine the whole concept behind switching from one *game* and going to the other. The key word here is "*game.*"

If these women are being truly honest with themselves, they should come to admit that unless the very first woman they get with, upon deciding to forego men, has delivered on the promise of Ms. Cinderella's dream of meeting someone that would deliver them from their pain the first time out (with no issue ever occurring that would create the same

121

kind of emotional highs and/lows they experienced with men), then regardless of whether they're with a man or a woman they still have to cover their bases… which means finding someone you can be happy with is an on-going process regardless of which sexual orientation a person may choose as their mate. And jf upon choosing to be with a woman, they find themselves still being in and out of relationships… then more than likely the problem is not the people they're with; the problem is the women themselves. And until they find a way to heal from the scars, it will remain an ongoing cycle.

SELF-HATE

When it comes to selecting a *player* to whom you give an application to apply for your team, most people tend to look for *players* right in their own backyard. Teams admire *players* that seem to know the ins and outs of the team's history and have a personal connection to wanting to be a part of continuing the team's legacy. In other words, it's natural for people to want to connect with people who share their cultural history and ethnic origin. In doing so, they're building on similar cultural experiences and values.

Everyone has preferences when it comes to what they consider to be attractive/unattractive, and no one can really control with whom they fall in love. This conversation is not about people who happen to meet someone outside of their culture and find a human connection to build on.

Where this conversation becomes deep is when your ability to choose someone from your ethnic background is thrown away due to your having internalized a traumatic experience you may have experienced while growing up (or witnessed someone else experience) and it has left you scarred to the point of coming to hate and reject your race/culture.

I'm not sure what happens for a person to arrive at a point where they're able to make a conscious decision to intentionally reject loving someone from their ethnic background. I assume this kind of self-hatred comes from a variety of places, such as repeated let-downs from men who share your ethnicity, being overexposed to someone else's perception of beauty and coming to see your own as unattractive, or simply deciding, for whatever reason, that men from your ethnic background seem to have a trait that makes them seem "inferior" to men of other ethnicities. Whatever the case may be, in order for you to have emotional balance you're going to have to eventually confront theses demons.

If you're a woman that's been able to convince yourself *males* outside of your ethnic group come with less "game play" than *males* from your culture, I'm here to announce that **ALL cultures have game** (the men and the women)! The difference you're observing when you encounter males from other cultures is not one that indicates there's no game being played. What you're observing is a cultural difference. And because you're observing as an outsider, it stops you from being able to immediately recognize *The Game* and the way it's being played, therefore rendering you blind to the obvious.

Yet, if you were to spend time talking and associating with women from that culture, you would quickly learn there's plenty of *Game* being run. Therefore, thinking you're going to be able to escape the inevitable by running somewhere else is merely a classic example of thinking the grass is greener on the other side of the fence. And no matter how far you run, it is inevitable: You too will have to **eventually cover ALL your bases if you're planning to stay in** *The Game* **to win**.

PREDATOR

Throughout history there have been many interesting depictions of women. And depending on where in history you decide to enter the conversation, you might run across images that paint them in a variety of ways.

Some images have been carefully sculpted to capture the tender side of women and depict them as caregivers, nurturers, and mothers. Others have chosen to reveal their spiritual beauty and have captured their image as pure, virtuous, and reverent. In contrast, at some point/time, someone began to recognize the full depth of women and switched the focus to their sex appeal; these are the images that show them as seductive, wanton, and sensual.

While these are all powerful images, all of them and more are merely a small glimpse of the complete picture of how truly versatile women are as *players in The Game* and the roles they have chosen to take on in a team setting. Despite the versatility and strength found in many of the stated images, most of them fail to compete with the image that depicts women as vampire predators who have decided it is better to prey on someone than to be the prey themselves.

You never know how a woman is going to react when her spirit has been broken. In some cases, she'll become reclusive and decide to stay away from men that remind her of the cause of her pain. In other cases, she might decide to internalize the hurt and take it out on herself through a variety of overindulgences such as overeating, overdrinking, and other extreme measures of self-infliction (such as attempting to find love through indulging in extreme sexually promiscuous, self-destructive behavior). However, in rare cases, a woman will internalize the pain to the point where she consciously decides to allow her compassionate side to wither like a raisin in the sun—and by doing so transforms into a hybrid that looks human, but behaves like an animal.

These are women that prefer to know that because they have been hurt, they are now the cause of other people's pain. They take great pride in creating the trap and selling the illusion of normalcy, but nothing about them is normal. Nor will it ever be until they begin to recognize that hurt/pain is a part of life and only through reflection of the lessons that came with the initial pain that made them become predators will they be able to grow, move on, and return to being a complete person.

When it's our time to suffer, we would all like to believe our pain is the greatest pain in the world and that no one has ever had to suffer the way we are. But it's not true. Everyone has had (and will have) pain; it is a natural part of life. What makes some people able to deal with their pain better than the next person is their ability to be open and honest about the mistakes they made, grow from them, and keep moving.

If you are a woman currently living as a *predator* and you've been able to convince yourself that hurting men (or people in general) is the only way you are going to be able to heal from the pain that was inflicted upon you, please know **you'll never heal this way**. You've got to find a way to get your joy back because that's what was taken from you.

There are plenty of silly people in the world and, unfortunately, as a woman (if you're not batting for the other side), many of the ones you deal with will be *males*, but ALL *men* aren't silly and ALL *men* aren't out to step on your soul. Sadly, you may have run into one (or two) that were *bad apples* (don't feel bad, you are not alone and you are not the first to have fallen victim to a *rogue baseman's* charm), but find the strength within yourself to be honest and reflective of what made you choose that kind of guy in the first place, and in doing so, I assure you that you will begin to find the lessons you needed to learn and begin to heal/grow.

On the other hand, if you are determined to maintain that you didn't make a mistake and you never played a part in the process that led up to your being hurt, sadly you're not ready to heal and eventually your actions as a *predator* will come back to you in ways you may find yourself unprepared to handle. **In the end, the only person that's going to lose in this *Game* will be YOU.**

PHALLUS ENVY... NO MALE ENERGY

Some women have had their spirits broken to the point where they've come to hate ALL male energy. Yet despite their content attitudes, ironically they have also come to reject femininity and consequently come to internalize many things associated with being a woman as a weakness. They see images that depict women as nurturing, virtuous, and sensual as pathetic attempts on behalf of men to limit the full scope of women's power. Some of these women once relished being feminine, but upon being hurt now find themselves beginning to feel at home in *sweats* with no make-up and waking around without their hair done. In addition, many of them proudly brandish their ability to curse like sailors and seem to bask in letting it be known to anyone that will listen, "I don't give a damn about male energy!"

It's never easy to identify the source of where such strong male rejection may stem; some say it's due to carrying hurt from early experiences of seeking to win male approval. Others say these women are suffering from *phallus envy* and secretly desire to have the power associated with having a penis. Whatever the case may be, it's always interesting to pay attention to how a lot of these women begin to take on the same characteristics they attribute to the male energy they despise. For example, in a work setting, some often abuse their power by trying to intimidate the people around them (especially male subordinates). In other settings (particularly social), they tend to be loud *know-it-alls* that are overly aggressive and prefer to be around people they can control.

If you're this kind of *female* and you seem to feel it's acceptable to reject feminine traits in order to replace them with masculine ones, you shouldn't find it hard to believe most *men* will tend to stay away from you. (**Note:** Notice I didn't say *"woman."* A *woman* takes pride in being **a woman** and a *female* that sees the traits that make *a woman a woman* as repulsive should not be forced to wear the title of being something she works so hard to reject.) To be frank, *this behavior is a little TOO macho for most men and we tend to see it as the equivalent of being with a guy*.

If you can't embrace being a woman, why would a guy want to embrace trying to make you feel like one? Again, there are always exceptions to the rule, so to say it will be completely impossible to find a man that will accept this would be an untrue statement. Yet I can assure you most men will give you ALL the space you need to be as macho as you like without committing to you. But because you are still a female (and you do still have womanly functions/parts) **don't be surprised to know men will still have sex with you;** most just won't take you seriously as anything but a *buddy*. Therefore, if your goal is to be actively engaged in playing *the man/woman Game,* you have to play the role and act the part.

FEMININE MALE

There are females that don't take their rejections of male energy to the same extreme as the previous example. Yet they still find ways to let it be known they have a problem with male energy. These women appear to be feminine in their outward appearance and embrace doing a number of things associated with being a female (such as being well manicured and very comfortable openly exuding traits of femininity). But underneath all of this outward appearance is a burning passion to reject anything associated with male energy.

If you're this kind of woman, to you I say: *"If a cat looks like a duck, walks like a duck, quacks like a duck, and acts like a duck…it's a DUCK!"* In other words, just because you look like a woman, but when you speak your words carry the undertones of a male, and when you walk, your walk turns into the strut of a man, and when it's time for your actions to speak, they show you inadvertently acting like a man…*you're simply a man in drag that's wearing a mask!* Therefore, my advice for you only makes sense if secretly you desire to have a long-term relationship with *a man* and you just haven't been able to figure out how to make it happen (which means you're planning to return to a point of liking men and the male energy that comes with them).

If this describes you, my advice is that you learn quickly that NO REAL MAN is going to ever want his woman to be tougher/harder than he is. So walking around acting like you have a phallus, and that yours is bigger than your man's, **will keep you locked out of the ball park and have your season tickets revoked!** Or it will keep you playing *The Game* in *the outfield* with men who specialize in playing games with women (especially women who seem to think they can change the nature of men). ANY *man* worth his weight in *manhood* is not going to take well to intimidation (especially from his woman), so you have to get back to learning how to embrace being comfortable with roles in relationships.

Note: I know some women can't stand to see the word "ROLE" and "RELATIONSHIP" mentioned in the same book—let alone the same sentence—but in The Game of Baseball, you're playing on a team. Therefore, you need to recognize that on teams people have ROLES. And if you're planning to be in a successful man/woman relationship, your

ROLE is to be happy being the woman in the relationship. If you can't handle it, keep doing what you've been doing and I hope it works out for you.

HEALING

When dealing with a broken spirit, it is never easy to tell what the final breaking point will be. However, it is important to know and identify, ways the spirit can be broken. All of the mentioned examples are but a small glimpse into how massive and diverse this topic can be. It is my hope that if you read an example that touched home, you will begin self-reflecting and try to make changes before it's too late.

Confronting pain that haunts us is not an easy task, and depending on the cause/level of the pain, some things go far beyond the journey of this book. If you have had an experience that rocked you to your core, left your spirit broken, or you want to begin to heal but the pain runs too deep, you should seek support from family, friends, or spiritual council. Healing may appear to be an uphill battle, but please know that through love, prayer, patience, and desire to recover...it is possible.

Don't let anyone deny you your right to happiness and peace of mind.

8ᵀᴴ INNING

HOME PLATE

As you read this, somewhere in the free world it's a beautiful day at the ballpark and the grass has never looked greener. The stadium seems to be pulsating with energy as the crowd sits on the edge of their seats, waiting for the next pitch. *The Game* has been an ongoing battle with both sides anxiously anticipating their opponent's next move. There are two outs in the bottom of the ninth and you have a leadoff on *third*. Clearly you are preparing to make your game-winning dash to h*ome plate* (which is sitting roughly ninety feet away). Although your head is in the game and you've never been more focused, it appears that everything is happening in *s...l...o...w* motion.

You see the pitch leaving the pitcher's hand and the bat being swung. You hear the roar of the crowd as they rise to their feet watching the action begin to

unfold. You see the ball begin to ascend in flight
towards the heavens as it connects with the bat. You
know the defense is running to catch the ball to keep
The Game in play and keep you stuck on *third*. Your
adrenaline is pumping, your instincts are taking over,
your legs kick in, and your body begins its dash
toward *home plate!* Your arms are pumping to give you
power/speed. Your heart is beating in unsynchronized
rhythms as your momentum carries you forward. The
ball has been retrieved and is being thrown toward
home plate. The catcher sees you coming and is in
position to greet you. His glove sits open as he
watches the ball being thrown towards *home* from
deep center field! You're determined you will score.
You've earned it by learning from your mistakes,
you've worked for it by learning to become a
consummate team player, you've prepared for it by
covering all your bases…and denial is not an option!

The ball is starting its final descent! The *catcher*
has one eye on you, one eye on the ball, and he's
covering *home plate,* trying to make sure you **earn** the
right to score! You see your chance to make it happen
and slide feet first into the plate. There's dust; the
crowd roars in excitement as you and the ball seem to
arrive at the plate at the exact same time! Everyone
waits for the dust to clear and to hear *the umpire's* final
call…the moment seems to take an eternity. Finally, he
waves his arms and his booming vociferous voice

says, "SAFE!!" The crowd takes to the field, your teammates rush out to embrace you, and in that moment…your life is forever changed!

THE CATCHER

If you've never taken the time to observe the game of baseball, you might not know the catcher is really the one that's calling the shots on the defense. Since he sits behind home plate, he not only has the full advantage of seeing the game unfold in front of him, he also plays an integral role in telling the pitcher what pitches to throw, when to walk players because they appear to an offensive threat, or how to pitch to players in a way that will strike them out. In addition, his main goal is to be the **gatekeeper of home plate** and to make sure no one crosses it without having to come through him to get there.

From the relationship perspective, *The Catcher* is not a *baseman*, yet his position is the most coveted spot in *The Game*…behind *home plate*. It is from there where he has been watching and taking notes on your growth as a *player*. He's positioned himself to have conversations with you as you stood at the plate waiting for the perfect pitch. And as the balls poured in pitch after pitch after pitch, he's been the one standing behind you, catching them and throwing back into the field to keep you at bat.

135

Because he's positioned behind you, when you initially step up to bat you don't immediately see his face, but you feel his presence and can hear his voice, and this lets you know he's real and will be waiting for you when you return from rounding the bases.

As an observer, he has an appreciation for watching you in your growth from
base to base and smiles inwardly when he sees how you were able to keep your head high when your *first baseman* didn't work out and your dreams of hitting a *homerun* seemed shattered. Yet instead of being broken by the experience, you took the time to reflect on the lesson, got back into training camp, recommitted yourself by working on your outlook/ personal development, and came back swinging.

When things didn't work out at *second*, he noticed how you never allowed yourself to give up on playing *The Game*, but instead kept your head high. He saw how you chose not to walk around blaming anyone for temporary set-backs, but again turned inward to build on lessons learned, opened your heart up to continue to grow, and moved forward knowing you were still preparing yourself for him.

From the time you hit *third*, he carefully watched to see whether or not you would become content with having made it further around the bases than most *players* ever will. He knows the comfort that comes with the *third baseman*, yet he never doubted you would make the decision to turn the corner full-steam ahead and press on toward *home plate*, carrying the lessons of all you learned with your spirit intact and ready to begin anew.

He marveled at how you instantly recognized his presence when you turned the corner and started to run toward *home* with all you had. He knew you had never seen his face, yet was confident you would know the comfort of his presence the moment you saw him.

As he watched you cover your bases, his mind flashed back to his own time at bat and how he too had been on a journey **preparing to greet YOU at** *home plate*.

He reflected on how he had grown from being a *male* who once played various positions on the field to now embracing being a *man* who's ready to be the epitome of a position player...**Your Husband**.

He knows as your husband, he no longer has the job of being a *baseman*. Therefore, he knows his job is to no longer break your heart, but to protect it as his own.

He's honored to know you two are no longer
individuals, but are now *a Team* **whose lives have
become one.** And in doing so, he knows his job is to
support you in your dreams/aspirations, and for you to
support him in his.

Although he is proud and holds his head high, he
recognizes there's strength in humility and knows
humbleness does not make him weak. Nor does false
chivalry make him brave. He values knowing there are
forces in the universe bigger than him, therefore he
finds strength in having a higher power to guide his
life so that you can trust him enough to guide and
nurture as your husband.

Your actions have shown him you are committed
to taking care of his sexual needs and he longs to
make sure he takes care of yours. And because you
have masterfully helped him tap into his *inner
Superman*, you have filled him with the desire to tear
down the baseball stadium, rename it so it bears your
name, and rebuild it either in your image...or to your
complete satisfaction. He truly craves you!

He respects your intellect and values your
opinions. He knows you are truly his equal and
welcomes you as his friend, his confidant, his lover,
and his companion; as a result, he has no problem

leading through his strengths or following you in yours.

He knows you will be an excellent mother and welcomes being the father of your children. He rejoices in knowing the children you have together will be a physical manifestation of your love and the children you have had separately will become testifiers of how dynamic you two are as a team.

He accepts you for who you are and asks only that you both remember to stay true to the lessons you learned while covering your bases. He has waited patiently for you to round *the bases* so he shuns the thought of ever being a *short-stop* in your life and **values knowing his journey has officially become yours, and yours officially his…until death do you part**.

What a game…welcome Home!

TIPS FOR SUCCESS

I know this goes against the grain of what you've been taught, but make sure you live for at least a year or two with ANY man you plan to stay in a long-term relationship with to gauge how responsible he is in his everyday actions as it relates to taking care of *the team* and carrying his weight (and make sure you take precautions so you DON'T get pregnant within that first year of living with him).

Always remember *The Game* you've played and the way you arrived at *home plate* is uniquely yours. Therefore it looks different from everyone else who has ever played *The Game*, and in order for you to make it to *the Hall of Fame*, you have to keep in mind that no two marriages are the same. What works as a game-winning strategy for you and your husband may not work for other people, so please remember to throw this kind of thinking out of your head.

What you will find that most successful marriages have in common is that they all contain two people who are committed to making it work, flexible in allowing their partners to continue to have personal growth/achievement, committed to staying true to the personal team rules they establish, enjoy being in one another's presence, and love one another to a point where they take pleasure in doing things that will allow them to see their partner happy.

9TH INNING

I bet you thought the journey was all over...not at all. Remember, *The Game of Baseball* is not over until the final out of the 9th inning (barring there is no overtime...but don't worry, I won't put you through that). Now is the time to introduce the one non-player I mentioned in the introduction, who would be critical to your development in *The Game*.

His job is one of the most underrated positions on the field, but he is the essential catalyst that makes the whole machine move. And without his direct presence/influence in *The Game,* you will never make it to the *Major Leagues*. Instead, you will be constantly playing street ball and learning to make up the rules as you go.

He's the stabilizer and has been calling the shots since you first entered *The Game*. It is his booming voice you've heard every time a pitch was thrown whether he felt it was *good* or *bad*. For example, it was he that yelled **"Strike!"** on the guy who was to have his first date with you, and neglectfully left you waiting by the door, without calling to say he would be late. **"Ball!"** was the word you would hear when a young man seemed to have a problem taking his hat off inside, or he never seemed to have enough strength to give a firm handshake while making eye contact. **"Foul!"** was his call when a guy seemed to play too rough with you, or was clueless about the direction he was moving towards in life. And whether you agreed or disagreed, you learned to be thankful he was there.

He's been standing behind you since day one when you first arrived at the ballpark, and he has patiently/intentionally taken his place on the field behind *the catcher* so he could watch every aspect of *The Game* unfold. His presence is one that **all** *players* in *The Game* respect and look to for final decisions.

To the rest of the world he is known as *"The Umpire,"* but to you...he's simply known as *"Daddy."* He is your father and you are his baby girl.

THE UMPIRE

In every game there has to be law and order, and in *baseball,* the *umpire* is the *gatekeeper.* His presence is so influential on how *The Game* unfolds that without him a woman is truly left to figure it out for herself, and the results of her lessons often come with a price no woman should have to pay. **Note:** I want to make sure I stress that although there's some romanticism behind the assumption that every girl will have their father in her life to play this role, the reality is that many won't/don't. In addition, I also want to make sure I strongly state that **EVERY DADDY IS NOT QUALIFIED TO BE AN UMPIRE**…but that's another book for another day.

Sadly, many women have been placed in situations where they have either come to see *the umpire* position as something they can get around and do without (thus this being the reason why so many of you reading this book never anticipated *the umpire* as a crucial position in *The Game*), or they have never had the option of having had the position filled. But the truth is *unless you have an umpire in your life in some capacity, your chances of making it to the Major League are slim to none.* In fact, you'll spend your time playing pick-up games and trying to live off your reputation of having once been a playground legend in your neighborhood, but you'll never advance to the next level of *The Game*.

As I stated when we first started this journey: "This *Game* has rules/structure, offensive/defensive tactics, coaches, and penalties." So it should come as no surprise when I state that not knowing or wanting to respect all aspects of *The Game* will cost you dearly. It should also not surprise you when I show you how not having someone who provides you with any structure in *The Game* will keep you from making it to the next level.

IMPORTANCE OF THE UMPIRE

Let's take a moment to really think about the crucial significance of the umpire's role in the game of baseball and reflect on how his absence really impacts the game:

Imagine being a naturally gifted ball player who has desires to go to the Major League, but you never played organized sports as a youth. However, you did manage to play pick-up games in the neighborhood, but never was able to get any real structure behind your development in the game. Therefore, all the rules you learned about the game came from street rules, where instead of playing nine solid innings with every position on the field being played by both sides, you generally played the game three men short. And instead of your game lasting nine well-fought innings, it only lasted three to five innings with every person not having a chance to bat, no umpires there to call the game, and no coaches there to guide you on strategy/technique to win.

And what if, because you learned to play street ball instead of having played organized ball, no one ever taught you about how to bunt the ball, how to make a sacrifice play, how to discover your strike zone as a batter, or how to hit a change-up pitch being thrown at you at 95 miles per hour. It is safe to say, while you might be the greatest player to have ever played in your neighborhood, because you really never played or learned to play any organized ball or learned how the game really works within a true complete team setting, you're ill-prepared to make it to the Major League and more than likely won't find yourself being a serious candidate among anyone's draft picks anytime soon.

In the relationship game, this example should help bring further clarity to why the role of *the umpire* is so crucial. Therefore, trying to act like you can get around having to learn to play within the rules of an organized team will have your dreams of making it to the majors cut short every time.

UMPIRE QUALIFICATIONS/ CERTIFICATION

I now want to take a moment to lay out the details of what qualifies a *man* to be an *umpire* because not every male is knowledgeable or respected enough around the *League of Men* to be called an *umpire*.

An *umpire* has to be well-rounded and truly a student of the game he is officiating. He doesn't have to be perfect (because no man is), but he has to be smart in his decision-making, responsible in his choices, openly accepting of his role/responsibility, and proud/responsible to know he is in fact *the gatekeeper of The Game* as well as the judge of crucial calls that have immediate to long-term effects on *the players* and *The Game's* outcome.

Although the natural *umpire* is assumed to be a girl's father, the reality is because so many *males* have not been willing to step up and take on their responsibilities, or they themselves have no clue about what being *a man* encompasses (another book for another day), this position can/has been filled by a number of other equally qualified men in a woman's life. Whether it's a stepfather, grandfather, an uncle, a brother, a cousin, or a surrogate who has stepped in to fill the role, the key is THERE HAS TO BE A

KNOWLEGABLE MAN WHO IS QUALIFIED/
CERTIFED in this position that fills it.

When it comes to having a *man* (notice I'm not
using the term *male*) fill the role of *umpire* (whether it's
your biological father or not), we have to be careful to
not assume all men have the same credentials. It's
important to point out that anyone can willingly give
themselves a title and walk around acting like they
know what they're talking about and pretending they
have a track record to prove it. However, too much is
on the line for you to operate off of someone's
imagination of what works and how they have
allegedly been successful in applying it to their lives.
Therefore, when it comes to verifying that an *umpire* is
in fact qualified/certified to be a suitable guide, there's
no better way to determine than taking a close
examination at his actual track record.

To put it plain and simple, a man can't be an
umpire if nowhere in his history of being a male has he
ever willingly taken on any responsibility for his
actions or recognized he has a responsibility to others
outside of himself. Therefore, if he has kids and has
not been actively involved in their lives, how the hell
is he going to be in a position to be an *umpire* and
guide you in yours?! If he has never found the time to
see the importance of serving others and being an
active member in his community, how can he in fact

know what that trait looks like in another man and advise you on what a *man of humility* and s*ervice* looks like? If he has a bunch of excuses as to why he's on his fifth marriage (**Note:** This is not to say people can't have made mistakes when they were in *The Game* and have possibly outgrown their mates and needed to move on....but, DAMN, THREE TO FIVE TIMES?!) maybe he's not the best person to guide you on what it takes to stay in *The Game*, especially when he seems to have a track record of making poor choices his damn self! If he has kids all over the world by every woman he ever slept with and he never seemed to find time to be involved in most of their lives because he allowed himself to be reduced to being a *"baby daddy"* instead of an *"engaged father,"* how can he possibly tell you what *a real man* looks like when his track record shows he's not one himself?!

All of this translates to mean that when you take the time to reflect and look at *your Game* and how it unfolds, you want to make sure you pay attention to what *man* in your life has been playing the role of *the umpire.* And if that man has in fact proven himself qualified/certified through his actions by having had his vision of successful relationships actually manifest in his life, then it's safe to say *he's a worthy umpire* and his advice and guidance should be cherished.

However, if after reflecting you come to realize you don't have this in your life and you never have, then my advice is to actively seek one out. I know that may sound easier said than done, but because *umpires* are *men* who pride themselves on being socially responsible and have no problem being active in their family/community, you actively seeking out their advice will be seen more as an honor than a burden. Therefore, don't let your shyness or insecurity about the matter deny you the chance to have this valuable resource in your life.

I also know it might be hard to admit your biological father fails/falls short of meeting the criteria of being a qualified or certified *umpire*, but again, in this *Game* the stakes are too high to sit around trying to correct his shortcomings; you have to move on. Unfortunately, sometimes that means you may have to look for this role to be filled by someone else outside of him who has a proven track record. No one ever said *The Game* would be easy, but I did say *The Game* will be played out one way or another, and you having insight into controlling how it plays out is/has been the main objective of our journey.

I hope you've enjoyed it as much as I have enjoyed embarking upon it with you. Good luck in your choices and no matter what...keep playing ball!!

POST-GAME WRAP-UP

SUMMARY OF THE GAME

Now that your journey is over and you've been empowered to control your fate as it relates to understanding the various stages you must go through to prepare for a successful long-term relationship, let's take a moment to make sure you walk away seeing the bigger picture of how to apply this information to your life.

As you have seen, in *The Game of Relationships,* I have pointed out three important stages you must go through in order to get prepared for marriage (assuming that's what you want in the end and why you're playing *The Game* to begin with). The key to your empowerment is making sure you begin applying your knowledge about these stages (and what they look/feel like) into your life by how you choose *the men* you let into your life.

Therefore, if you know you are currently on *first base*, trying to date a guy that's on *third* will not work for you. He's out of your league and you simply haven't had enough time in *The Game* to sustain him.

On the other hand, let's say you're at *third* and you run across a guy that's clearly a *second baseman*. Trying to make him a *third baseman* is not going to get you what you want. In the end, he'll simply be a *second baseman* playing out of position and failing miserably because you're trying to force him to be something that he's not. In time, he may eventually become a *third basemen,* but it won't be because you forced him to; it will be because he put in the time and gained the proper amount of experience/skills under his belt to play the position, which means this might take years. Therefore, unless you're planning to wait and let nature take its course naturally with his evolution, you might want to leave him alone and focus on someone that's on your current base.

If you find that you are always dealing with *outfielders* but you're trying to get to a point where you're on track to play the game in the infield so you can get on a *marriage track,* you now know what you have to do.

If you are the woman that's always attracting *short-stops* and you never seem to know what it is about you that seems to continuously invite this kind of energy, you now know and can make a conscious decision to change your thinking so you can attract something new. Plus, you now know that if you have been dealing with a *short-stop* and have been trying to figure out why you can't get him to really commit, it's because he's not really a *baseman* to begin with. **Remember, the real *Game* is being played on first, second, and third.**

Also, always bear in mind that no two teams are the same, so as you build your team, keep in mind that your team/game is uniquely yours and that although the rules for *The Game* are universal, the structure and politics of the team are not. That means what works for you and your mate may not be what works for your girlfriend and her mate, your sister and her mate, or your mother and your father. This is what makes *The Game* so special; although new players will always come and go, *The Game* will always generally remain the same. So pick and choose how YOU want to play it.

OUT OF THE NORM

I know a lot of what I said goes against the grain of what many of society's traditional institutions teach, **but my approach is more about applying common sense and practicality versus theory and tradition**. Therefore, when I advise you to have sex with your mate before marriage (as previously stated, you naturally want to exude some common sense in your choices) and live with a man you have a serious interest in for at least one year before making any life-changing commitments, this is more about your getting a chance to really see how this person fits you and how he accepts responsibility in his day-to-day life. And if after a year or so you have seen all you need to see…feel free to move forward accordingly. I would rather you find out you made a mistake and be able to move on quickly than have you make a costly commitment only to discover it wasn't worth it.

The most important thing for you to understand about covering *the bases* is that **the positions are real** and by knowing where you are in *The Game* at all times, you'll know exactly who you should (or should not) be dealing with. If you find that you're not dealing with someone that's on the same *base* as you, you now have the power to make a conscious decision to let him go so you can move on or to simply keep playing *The Game* out of position and learn your lessons the hard way. **The bottom line is the choice is**

now in your handsand you can no longer say you
didn't know.

HALL OF FAME

Every player that has ever played the game of baseball, and was worth their weight in gold, has always played with a sense of purpose and determination to go down in history as one of the best to have ever worn the uniform. This stands true for relationships as well.

Most sane people never play *The Game* saying to themselves: "*I want to be known as the biggest loser to have ever stepped foot in a relationship. In fact, let me see what I can do to jack up every single facet of my relationship and run everyone the hell away from me as quickly and as often as possible!*" Instead, I think it's safe to say that most people want just the opposite and would like to have long, successful relationships that not only enhance their lives but enhance the lives of others around them as well.

With all of this being stated, it is now time to introduce the *Hall of Fame* and what it takes to get inducted.

CREDENTIALS

Just like you can't have played the game of baseball for 1 – 3 years and find yourself on someone's ballot for being inducted into the Baseball Hall of Fame, is the same way you can't have had a successful relationship for 1 - 3 years and find yourself being nominated for the *Relationship Hall of Fame*.

Hall of Fame players are proven *gamers*. They are people who have found a way to overcome obstacles that were thrown in their path countless times and still managed to stay in *The Game* contributing to making *the team* better. They are people who weathered the storm when the team sucked and no one really came to the ballpark. They are people who, when the funds were low (and cuts had to be made), gave up part of their salary to keep the team afloat until things turned around. Hall of Famers are people who, when the joy of playing *The Game* had hit a personal low and *the team* seemed to be on the verge of being torn apart, they found a way to reinvent themselves and remain at the top of their game as consummate team players who continued to elevate their game through their relentless drive to win!

In other words, Hall of Fame Players are people who have given their blood, sweat, and tears to make the team strong and in the end found a way to turn their sweat equity into 20-plus years of love and prosperity.

The key to making it to the Hall of Fame is your track record of success, what you contributed to others, how successful they went on to become (mainly your children and possibly your grandchildren), whether or not you gave more to *The Game* than you took from it, and whether or not you put the time in to get there. **Note:** This is not to say that some people can't be serious candidates for the Hall of Fame even though they fall short of the time requirement (i.e., widow/widowers), but they are on a case-by-case basis and their contributions will have to be something really special to get around the bare minimum time requirement.

HALL OF FAME CONTROVERSY

There are some that argue you can't make the Hall of Fame if there was no mental, physical, spiritual, and emotional fulfillment in your relationship. They argue this is not acceptable because if your reason for staying was really only for the sake of seeing the kids happy (yet YOU were miserable), then you really didn't have a successful relationship; you were merely a prisoner of circumstance that opted to stay and suffer.

Whereas I can clearly see how one might arrive at this conclusion, I have to take a moment to talk about what makes a Hall of Fame player special. It's not their ability to have stayed merely for the sake of staying, but their ability to have stayed and still been able to produce quality from a bad situation. Case in point, let's say the person was in a situation where the marriage was truly a bad fit on a number of levels, but despite this they found a way to stay for the sake of their children and was able to produce kids that grew up to be emotionally stable, mentally balanced, and well-rounded, contributing members to society who went on to have successful relationships of their own without having emotional relapses of horrid childhood memories...I would have to say this person is truly Hall of Fame material.

On the other hand, let's take the same scenario and instead of producing balanced, contributing members to society, they produced offspring that are emotionally dense and tend to leave every person they ever tried to be in a relationship with emotionally drained from trying to ward off all the evil spirits of their haunted childhood. Well, it's safe to say because their contribution has taken away from *The Game* more than they added to it, they have not earned the right to be in the Hall of Fame.

KIDS... THE DETERMINING FACTOR

Kids can be great factors in determining whether or not your team is Hall of Fame material, but not the only factor. They are a great factor because they are a reflection of your values and work ethic from 20 years of marriage. After the age of 20, we can now see what your offspring look like in the bigger picture of society and whether or not they are balanced, contributing members.

Obviously all couples don't go on to have children, but if during their time together they have loved deeply, prospered emotionally/mentally/spiritually, and have truly been enjoying their journey through life as best friends for the last 20-plus years, I would have to say they deserve to be in the Hall of Fame as well. **Note:** I'm sure you're wondering why I keep making the bare minimum for entry into the Hall of Fame 20 years. This is not a random number. I chose it because in the U.S prison system, one life sentence is 20 - 25 years (not that I'm comparing marriage or successful long-term relationships to prison). Therefore, it only makes sense that if you have successfully been with someone for 20-plus years in a society where the average marriage might last only 15 years, you obviously have found a way to elevate your game and rise above the odds.

FINAL REFLECTION

Now that we know what it takes to get here, ask yourself: How many *Hall of Fame teams* do you know? If your answer is "none," taking a moment to reflect on this and asking yourself what seems to be the problem might save you from a similar fate. If no one in your family or immediate surroundings has ever been able to have a lasting relationship, reflecting on why will help you avoid their pitfalls. In addition, this book has been written with you in mind to help offer you a solution on how to break away from the path and start anew. Hopefully you have been an astute student of *The Game* and really took to heart the advice of this book by incorporating it into your life.

Regardless, I wish you well on your journey and hope you always remember to **play** *The Game* **to the best of YOUR ability**. Who knows? In 20 - 25 years, hopefully someone will have nominated you as one of the best to have ever played *The Game* and you'll be preparing to take your place in the Hall of Fame right where you always deserved/wanted to be.

On the other hand, if when reflecting you discover you know plenty of *Hall of Fame teams* (and have access to their players), be sure to seek them out to see what they did to get there. For further clarity and validation of my message, check to see if any of them actually followed the blue print I laid out in this book. If upon doing your investigation you discover they did apply many of the things I pointed out, then you know what you have to do to get there as well. And if you happen to discover they didn't apply any of the rules I spoke of (although I seriously doubt this will be the case), then ask yourself if their approach seems feasible for you. If you decide that it is, I still wish you the best and hope to one day see your name mentioned as one of the best to have ever worn the uniform.

About The Author

Shon Watts is an educator/visionary with an honest writing style that pulls readers into having personal journeys of reflection. He has a Master's degree and credits the College of Education for encouraging him to seek ways to continue educating outside of the classroom. As founder and CEO of Up Close and Personal Publications, he is dedicated to producing books that help readers expand their horizons, challenge antiquated beliefs, reflect on life lessons, and grow. He lives in the United States.

Contact information: <u>Shonwatts@gmail.com</u>

Made in the USA
Lexington, KY
11 February 2011